Also available at all good book stores

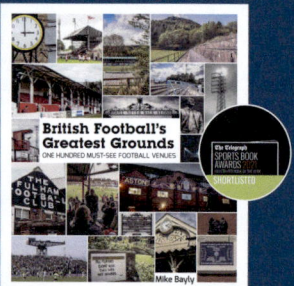

9781785316470

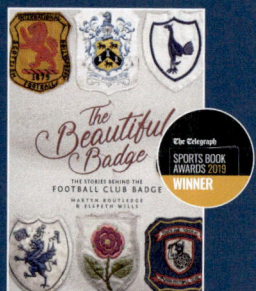

9781785313929

9781785315602

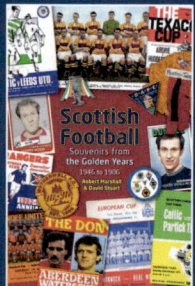

9781785318641

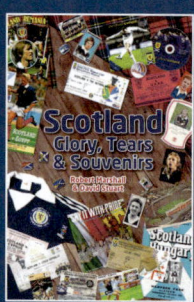

9781785313318

9781785315459

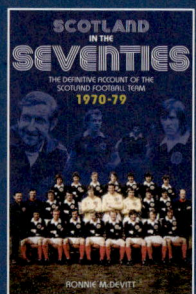

9781785314391

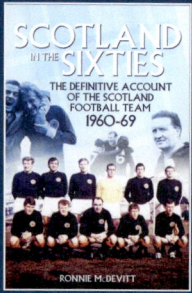

9781785311802

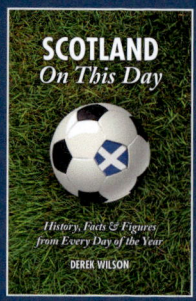

9781905411832

Scotland's
Lost Clubs

Scotland's
Lost Clubs

Giving the Names You've Heard,
the Story They Own

Jeff Webb

First published by Pitch Publishing, 2021

Pitch Publishing
A2 Yeoman Gate
Yeoman Way
Worthing
Sussex
BN13 3QZ
www.pitchpublishing.co.uk
info@pitchpublishing.co.uk

A CIP catalogue record is available for this book
from the British Library.

ISBN 978 1 78531 862 7

Typesetting and origination by Pitch Publishing
Printed and bound in Great Britain by TJ Books, Padstow

Contents

To Claudine and Vienna. Thank you so much for putting up with me being physically attached to my laptop for what feels like years. Also, thanks to Paul and Jane at Pitch for being so understanding about my what feels like never-ending delays. Finally, thanks to Spence and Andy for putting up with me moaning about word counts at every pint we had, and to the guys at Forgotten Clubs, Phil and Ross especially, without whom I don't think I'd ever have had the belief in myself to go out and write an actual book.

Introduction

THE THINKING behind this book was simple. I absolutely love Scotland and Scottish football. Scotland is a country of massive extremes: the schemes, tenements and industrial smog of Glasgow and the Central Belt at the one extreme, and the unending beauty of the Highlands and islands at the other. It has a history of being unsure of itself, even before the Crowns of England and Scotland came together. Scotland until 1998 was even more uneasy; it had no parliament and the only stage it would be able to show itself on as something separate was through its sport. This meant that in Scotland, more so than anywhere else, football players became the folk heroes. The footballer became the same to Scotland as a bullfighter is to Spain, as a tenor is to Italy and as an actor is to the USA. He became a true working-class hero.

After 1603 when the English handed their throne over to King James VI of Scotland, things changed. The people had lost their king, and even though in Scotland loyalties had always been a mix of ancient agreements and friendships that had lasted centuries, the House of Stuart had ruled Scotland since 1371.

In 1603 when the English invited King James VI to London to take the throne, things looked as if they were about to change, with peace being brought between the two kingdoms as they would both be viewed as equals. However, things are never black and white when it comes to these two countries. When the Scots waved away their king in 1603, none would have believed it would take until 1633 for them to see him again. In fact, it wasn't even their king anymore; King James VI of Scotland soon became King James I of England, and history now remembers him solely as that. In 1625, King James VI died and was replaced by his second son Charles.

King Charles I, who was born in Dunfermline Palace in 1600, hadn't visited Scotland since his early childhood. He was declared King of Scotland, England and Ireland in 1625, although he was only crowned King of England and Ireland in that year, because the Scots refused to send Scottish Crown Jewels to London for the coronation. Finally, after eight years of negotiations, which mostly consisted of the King demanding the jewels be sent to London and the Scottish Parliament saying no they won't, an agreement was reached for the King to come to Edinburgh to be crowned King of Scotland. When in 1633 King Charles I came to Edinburgh it was a nation that was a lot poorer than the one he had left, but also one that was more curious. Scotland had throughout its history learned to live without a king and it kept plodding along just fine. As Charles made his way along the Royal Mile to St Giles' Cathedral in Edinburgh, he was a matter of great interest to the people lining the route. Things were uneasy from the start as the Scottish nobles were feeling pushed aside and viewed as an inconvenience by the King, which led to a tense coronation. To add to this, Charles demanded that the ceremony use the Anglican rite rather than the traditional ceremony the Scots had carried out for over a century.

Soon after the ceremony in 1633, King Charles fell out with the Scottish Parliament. This wasn't uncommon with Charles, but in 1637 things took a turn. The King ordered that all the kirks in Scotland should use a new prayer book, which was pretty much the *English Book of Common Prayer*. As the King hadn't consulted the Kirk or Parliament, this didn't go down as well as he had expected. There were riots in Edinburgh, Perth and Stirling. Ministers had rotten food, stones and faeces thrown at them. One minister in a kirk outside Edinburgh managed to keep the peace by standing in his pulpit preaching with the help of two loaded pistols either side of the Bible. Finally, in November 1638, the General Assembly of the Church of Scotland condemned the new prayer book and removed the bishops placed by the King from their posts.

This action led the King to start a war with the country of his birth because he feared his power was slipping. The Bishops' War, as it became known, was a military disaster for the King. He had spent most of his own money to save having to recall Parliament. When he got to Berwick-upon-Tweed he became reluctant to go to battle, knowing how outnumbered his troops were and how determined the Scots were to defend their Church and heritage. Instead, the King signed the Treaty of North Berwick in which he strengthened his position as King of Scotland but also reaffirmed the strength of the Scottish Parliament and the General Assembly of the Church of Scotland.

With the humiliating scaling down from the King during the Bishops' War and subsequent fallout, the wheels were in motion for the English Civil War between a king who believed he ruled directly from God and a parliament that had barely been called during his reign. When things finally came to a head in 1642, the Scots raised an army to support their king. They fought at the opening exchanges in the Battle of Powick Bridge, just outside the city of Worcester, in September 1642. When on 30 January 1649 King Charles I was beheaded for treason in London, the Scots straight away declared his son Charles II as King of Scotland. The Scots again came to their king's aid when he needed to raise an army. This army was defeated at the Battle of Worcester in September 1651, during which the Scots lost over 2,000 men. The King, after this defeat, escaped the city and went into exile until the restoration of 1660.

Even after everything the Kingdom of Scotland did for both Charles I and Charles II, it did the country no favours. By the time King Charles II died in 1685, Scotland was becoming increasingly isolated from Europe. When King James VII of Scotland and II of England came to the throne the world was a very difficult place. James was a committed Catholic, which was at direct odds with the Protestant views of the country. Finally, in 1688, William of Orange and his wife Mary were invited to take the throne. During the inevitable war that followed, William beat James at the Battle of the Boyne in 1691 to confirm his position.

In Scotland things were, as now, split. Most in the Lowlands were happy with this new Protestant king. However, in the Highlands an army was raised based on old loyalties to the House of Stuart. The army, which won the Battle of Killiecrankie, was soon defeated by a much smaller force at the Battle of Dunkeld. These two battles, as well as the massacre of Glencoe in 1692, made the country even more uneasy with the treatment it was receiving from this new king.

In 1695, with the country having limited capital and noticing that other European countries were making their wealth from colonies, Scotland tried to set up a colony in Panama. The Scottish government passed an act that created the Bank of Scotland to raise the funds required. This was an attempt to start an empire to allow the nation to become richer and more prosperous. However, it was always destined to fail. The ships that set sail were criminally unprepared and the people who sailed had no experience for the weather conditions they faced. For example, they took over 300 woollen undergarments for a colony on the equator, amongst countless other mistakes. Then came the English colonies in the area, which at the start promised to help the fledgling Scots; however, they quickly turned and left them to their fate.

The final nail in the coffin came in 1699 when the Scots took to raiding Spanish ships in the area. This led to the Spanish raising a force of 500 men to take the lands the Scots held. When they marched in, they found that the land was all but abandoned and of the 2,000 settlers that left Leith in 1695 only 150 would see their homeland again. Most had fallen to disease. As a result, the colony was officially abandoned in 1699. This failure had cost Scotland half a million pounds at the time, effectively bankrupting the country to such a degree that it was a main factor behind the Act of Union in 1707.

In 1702, Queen Anne took the throne, and from the start an Act of Union between England and Scotland was her priority. By 1705 she had ordered that negotiations begin between the parliaments. Eventually, in May 1707, the two nations joined in an Act of Union that has kept the nations linked ever since.

The 18th century was a time when being Scottish was viewed with suspicion. After the rebellions of 1715 and 1745, things that made Scotland its own country were frowned upon in some cases, but in most were outright banned by the government. By the end of the century things that were Scottish were becoming British. The most telling sign of Britain and England being all but the same thing was the Battle of Trafalgar in 1805. Famously, in the sea battle that turned the tide of the Napoleonic Wars, Nelson sent a flag signal from HMS *Victory* saying: 'England expects that every man will do his duty.' Not Britain, not the United Kingdom, not even the King, but England.

Scotland had become an interesting place to visit by the 19th century, a place of outstanding beauty, but its pride as a nation had been blunted. However, things did start to change by the second decade of the century. In 1814, Sir Walter Scott published *Waverley*, and while the novel itself isn't the reason why pride came back to Scottish people, it was a bestseller and the perspective it gave was one that showed that the lines between loyalty to the Crown and pride in being Scottish weren't necessarily polar opposites, and that during the uprisings in the 18th century they were in some cases not as black and white as the government at the time would have you believe. It showed that being Scottish within Britain could be a thing to have pride in. Scott's works, compounded with the nationalism that Burns had written about 40 years earlier, started to make the Scottish people proud of their homeland once again.

As the 19th century wore on, Scots became prouder of their nation. Most of this came from military commanders and industrial leaders through the first half of the century making great strides within the Empire. However, following on from the horror of the Crimean War, the world had a strange sense of peace. Technology was always still coming through, but the main work had been done and the giant strides had turned somewhat into small steps. Railways made the country a smaller place and journey times changed from weeks to hours. Mass production took over from cottage industry and cities sprung up where villages once held strong.

With the British Empire at a sense of peace, the need for a large standing army started to drift. This, combined with mass industry squeezed into small cities, started to provide people with time on their hands. Not much spare time, but some. It was in this background that football started to come to the fore. In 1855 Sheffield Football Club became the first club to take up a sport of kicking a leather into a goal at either end of a pitch, with England's top private schools also using it as a method of preventing the students from sinning. Sheffield Football Club brought the game to the working-class public domain. As it didn't require the weather, equipment or pitch sizes of cricket, and as it was a fast-flowing, time-limited game compared with cricket, it became increasingly popular.

Over the next decade various modes of the sport were played in towns and cities throughout the country. The game passed easily from town to town with the railways and the navvies who helped build them. By 1860 unofficial teams started to pop up around the land. Most were encouraged to play by companies, industries and even the Church as a way of keeping their workers and congregations from the moral dangers of alcohol.

In Scotland it wouldn't be until 1867 that the first real association club would be formed, when on 9 July 1867, at 3 Eglinton Terrace, Queen's Park Football Club came into existence. The importance of this club can't be over-stated. People often say that the weight of history can bear down on people. This, as you will soon learn, is something that every player will feel when they pull on the black-and-white hoops of the famous Spiders.

Queen's Park's importance within football, not just in Scotland but throughout the world, is massive and sadly often misunderstood or outright ignored. Famously, Bob Crampsey, the writer, broadcaster and journalist, once compared the role of Queen's Park in football to that of the Royal and Ancient Golf Club of St Andrews in golf.

As you will read time and time again throughout this book, the role that Queen's played in the expansion of the game in Scotland is second to none. The club in the early years of football in Scotland were the dominant force, the elder statesmen of Scottish football with an aura of respectability and authority about them, but also a true sense of just playing for the pure enjoyment of the sport. The club's motto is *Ludere Causa Ludendi*, which translates as

'To Play for the Sake of Playing'. The club, like Corinthian FC from London, stuck strictly to the theory that by being amateurs you are playing for enjoyment and not for monetary gain. Queen's would stick to this principle for over 150 years until 2019, when after the sale of Hampden Park to the Scottish Football Association (SFA), Queen's needed to adapt to the modern era. So finally, on 14 November 2019, a vote was passed by 91 per cent of the members of Queen's Park to turn pro. This meant that the club could finally collect transfer fees for players that they had helped launch the careers of.

The importance of Queen's Park can only really be understood if you look at the numbers. They have won the Scottish Cup ten times, which even today puts them third on the overall list. This probably says more about the dominance of Celtic and Rangers than Queen's, but it's still impressive for a team who have not appeared in a final since 1900. They even appeared in two English FA Cup finals, losing both to Blackburn Rovers. They have also won the Glasgow Cup four times, the Glasgow Merchants' Charity Cup eight times and in 1899 shared the Sheriff of London's Charity Shield with England's Aston Villa, who were in the middle of winning four league titles in five years.

In any book about Scottish footballing history, the role of Queen's Park needs to be explained. The club was vital in expanding the game through touring the country and playing against any team that requested a friendly. From Fort William to Wick, and from Dumfries to Eyemouth, the club would facilitate any team that wanted to play them, all in the name of expanding the game throughout the country. As time has gone on, people, the story of the club's role in creating the SFA, the Scottish national team and even the passing game has long been forgotten.

Queen's Park Football Club Honours
Scottish Cup winners: 1874, 1875, 1876, 1880, 1881, 1882, 1884, 1886, 1890, 1893
Runners-up: 1892, 1900
English FA Cup runners-up: 1884, 1885
Scottish second tier: 1922/23, 1955/56
Scottish third tier: 1980/81
Scottish fourth tier: 1999/00, 2020/21
Play-off winners: 2006/07, 2015/16
Glasgow Cup: 1889, 1890, 1899, 1946
Glasgow Merchants' Charity Cup: 1877, 1878, 1880, 1881, 1883, 1884, 1885, 1891

Founding of the League

WHEN QUEEN'S Park were formed in 1867, clubs started to pop up all around the country, and taking their lead from England, they put an advert out to ask fellow clubs to join them in creating a Scottish Football Association in 1873.

The idea came from not so much the English FA but rather the FA Cup. The FA in England was created in 1863 to form an organisation that would standardise the rules of the game but nothing more. Then in 1871 the idea came to create a challenge cup to be played by teams throughout England.

With the success of the FA Cup creating proper competitive matches between teams and seeing the crowd numbers increase, it became clear to the committee at Queen's Park that a similar version in Scotland would be a sensible manoeuvre. So, on 13 March 1873, seven teams – Queen's Park, Clydesdale, Vale of Leven, Dumbreck, Third Lanark, Eastern and Granville – plus a letter of intent to join from Kilmarnock, met to form the SFA. During the meeting they resolved:

The clubs here represented form themselves into an association for the promotion of football according to the rules of The Football Association and that the clubs connected with this association subscribe for a challenge cup to be played annually, the committee to propose the laws of the competition.

With that statement the SFA and Scottish Cup were formed. The SFA would take over the running of the Scotland national team, which had recently played the world's first-ever official international football match, held at the West of Scotland Cricket Club ground, Hamilton Crescent in Partick, on 30 November 1872. The 4,000 spectators that attended that first international were treated to a 0-0 draw between the two teams, but even so, history had been made. The Scotland team that day wore the dark blue jerseys of Queen's Park, from which all 11 players were drawn, the only time one club has provided all 11 Scotland players.

With the success of both the Scottish Cup and the FA Cup, clubs began to get restless at having a limited number of competitive matches every season. They were beginning to see a steep increase in crowd numbers, which by default saw a big increase in money coming in. However, it was clear that this increase was mainly for competitive matches rather than friendlies, and yes, while each county and city had a variety of cup competitions, it was the national competitions that seemed to attract the greatest number of supporters through the gates.

Gradually, after nearly two decades in which the number of clubs taking part multiplied tenfold and professionalism was finally permitted in England in 1885, the clubs in England wanted a change, to guarantee more concrete fixture lists and to have more matches. This would mean more money coming through the turnstiles, hence more cash to attact the best players available, which it was hoped would mean greater success on the playing field. So, led by Scotsman William McGregor of Aston Villa, 12 of the top clubs met at the Royal Hotel in Manchester to form the English Football League on 17 April 1888.

In Scotland the clubs watched on carefully to see how this league would play out. Finally, after watching the success of the first season in England, the clubs in Scotland started to push for a league of their own to be formed. Eventually, the secretary of Renton FC, a Mr Peter Fairly, sent the following letter to 14 clubs in Scotland:

> *Gentlemen,*
> *You are requested to send two representatives to attend a meeting to be held in Holton's Commercial Hotel, 28 Glassford Street, Glasgow, on Thursday 20th March at 7.30p.m. Yours truly*
> *(signed) Peter Fairly, secy.*
>
> *BUSINESS:– To consider the question of organising League matches in Scotland.*

Both Clyde and, most interestingly, Queen's Park didn't attend. Queen's made it public knowledge that they believed the forming of the league was simply a pretence to bring in professionalism to the Scottish game, which they believed would lead to many of the smaller teams from outside of the city being forced out of the game and marginalised. While the historic club were willing to be pushed aside, their foreboding was correct, as by 1900 six of the original 12 were no longer playing league football.

The 12 that did turn up to the meeting were Abercorn, Cambuslang, Celtic, Cowlairs, Dumbarton, Heart of Midlothian, Rangers, Renton, St Bernard's, St Mirren, Third Lanark and Vale of Leven. The minutes from that first meeting are now sadly long gone. However, reporters at the time could attend and a journalist from the popular sports paper at the time, *Scottish Sport*, was at the meeting. This is the full extract from *Scottish Sport*, from 22 March 1890, when that first meeting to create the Scottish Football League (SFL) took place.

With the League Agitators

Tis Thursday night. The modest little 'alarm' on the far-off corner of the sanctum has claimed the hour of seven. Sport has just gone to press, and the P.D. has left me alone, leaving behind a hideous caricature of old 'scissors and paste'. A bundle of unopened editorial communications lie on the desk usually occupied by 'Ye Journiemanne' while everything around is a chaos of confusion and darkness. I was about to depart when the word 'League', written in bold characters on the margin of a rejected pile of manuscripts, arrested my attention. Look at the word again, write it slowly, ponder over its significance, and mayhap similar feelings of curiosity and excitement will pervade you as they did me. Suddenly I recollected that the epistle heretofore mentioned referred to a meeting to be held in the short space of half-an-hour, for the purpose of discussing and, if possible, establishing a football League in Scotland. Here was a chance not to be lost, and in the language of the melancholy member of our staff, I wended my way to Holton's Hotel 'with mingled feelings of pleasure and regret' – pleasure at the probable privilege of listening to proposals, fraught with the most momentous issues, with just the possibility of a direct revolt to usurp the power of the institutions which has so long, so honourably, and so faithfully guided the destines of Scotch football; regret at the not too inviting prospect of undergoing the humiliating process of being 'chucked out'. My perturbed state of mind was somewhat relieved when I discovered I was the first arrival. Something new in my experience this, so take a note of it. Here, in the rather plain and cheerless apartment at the far end of the lobby, free from the intrusion of the usual 'commercial' intruder, was the trysting place. A small wooden table, with five wooden chairs to keep it company, were arranged almost in the centre of the room, and immediately behind the chairs three wooden school forms, with no resting place on which to lean a wearied back, were arranged. The materials for a fire were in the fire-place, but there was no light. I was beginning to despair of visitors, when in pops the burly, if not commanding proportions, of Mr P. Campbell of Renton, along with several inferior (in bulk, of course) co-workers. At the suggestion of one of these a light was applied to the fire, and the aspect of affairs changed completely.

With the exception of the Queen's Park and Clyde, all the clubs circulated sent two representatives, and quite an air of importance and influence attached to the gathering, as the following list will show, viz.:- Third Lanark, Celtic, Rangers, Cowlairs, St Mirren, Abercorn, Renton, Dumbarton, Vale of Leven, Cambuslang, St Bernard's and Heart of Midlothian.

Mr Lawrence (Dumbarton) was asked to preside, and, in doing so, stated he yielded to the desires of the meeting in this line of conduct. So far as his club was concerned, he was not present in an official capacity, prepared to vote on whatever proposal might be adopted. He administered a mild exhortation to his audience to be reasonable, dispassionate, and not too easily swayed by the arguments which would be adduced in favour of the proposal. The Dumbarton were prepared to support it on the lines he indicated at a later stage of the proceedings.

At the request of the Chairman, Mr Graham (Rangers), as taking the initiative, rose and propounded his views. These may be briefly summed up as a protest against the existing cup tie arrangement, the derangement of the fixture card, and the frequent class of matches they were compelled to play. He further declaimed the impression which had gone abroad that the Renton were agitating for the introduction of professionalism in any shape or form. This was to be distinctly understood, and he was conscious those present would give Renton every credit for their loyalty to the very spirit of amateurism. The invitation to participate in the proceedings was extended to all, and Mr J. H. McLaughlin, in his eloquent and deliberate style, stated the only parallel they had to go upon was the Football League in England, an institution which had created a greater interest than formerly existed in the game across the border. The League has the advantage of a first-class and attractive array of fixtures, without the spirit of acrimony or rough play, which was conspicuous in cup tie engagements. Mr John Thomson (Third Lanark) was also in sympathy with the movement, as being beneficial all round.

Mr Reynard (Cambuslang), whose face throughout the evening was wreathed in smiles, now rose, and with inspiration derived from the exhilarating effects of a cigarette, stated his club had discussed the matter in committee, and he was there by invitation to hear and report all that passed. The Cambuslang were quite prepared to support a qualifying competition. He considered it a very great hardship that clubs such as the status as Queen's Park and Celtic should be drawn together in the first round. Once out of the ties the club was insufficiently supported, and the sooner something was done to maintain the interest the better.

A look of the tenderest sympathy with the object under discussion overspread the facial development of the representatives of the Vale of Leven, as the chairman politely requested his opinion. The eloquence of previous speakers, however, seemed to have overawed him completely, for a modest assent of approval with what was going on was all that could be eliminated from the delegate of the famous club on the banks of the Leven. Things certainly were looking up, and everyone seemed delightfully contented as one after another orated on the eventualities of the future. When Mr J. Mellish (Rangers) got to his legs, the interest heightened, and anxious anticipation was depicted on the faces around. One whose knowledge and splendid powers of organisation would be invaluable to the movement under weight would surely carry conviction. I thought, and eagerly I hung – so to speak – on the utterances of the representative of the SFA. Without lacking the firmness, regularity of speech, and air of conscious ability which usually characterises his appearances, the speaker began. I was disappointed with his short speech, probably because I had expected a longer one, and probably because he had nothing in the way of originality to enrapt the attention. My feelings must have been akin to the hot-headed politician, whose favourite hero had only bowed from the railway carriage. Mr Mellish's words, as I have said, were few, but were those of a diplomatist. In conjunction with

Mr Wilton, he had come there to listen and report. Provided the League was got up in a proper way, and for the benefit and furtherance of Scottish football, he could see no harm in the departure, but it <u>must</u> be <u>strictly</u> amateur and recognise the SFA as the governing body. He had no instructions to act definitely.

The next speaker – Mr George Henderson, whose long connection with the Cowlairs instinctively made me grasp my pencil and hurriedly turn the leaves of my note-book, in case I should omit some sentence of infinite moment and purport – began, 'well, Mr Chairman and gentlemen, we have had this matter before our committee and fully discussed it, and our recommendation is in favour of a League'. This in all one breath, and with a flow which conveyed to me the impression that he was afraid his tongue might drop out ere he completed his peroration. 'They had got up such a thing in England, and it would be to the advantage of clubs in Scotland to follow suit. The question of gates would be required to be settled when the League was formed. We are quite prepared to settle definitely any proposal that might be adopted, provided it was organised in proper form, and looking to the interests of the Association. We hope the Association would grant a qualifying competition and it would be a very good thing, indeed.' (Cheers.) With wonted timidity, and leaning hard on the handle of a stout umbrella, Mr Smith (Heart of Midlothian) 'modestly addressed himself to speech'. The Hearts never did seriously discuss this matter, or consider its details, but they were just in this position – ready to go with the times.

Somebody whispered Mr Lamb (St Bernard's) had just come in, and though the Queen's Prizeman said, looking in the direction of the door, 'Mr Lamb', that individual answered ne'er a word, but kept fondly gazing at the ring on his little finger, in the hope evidently of gleaning something bright.

One volunteer is worth three pressed men any day. So thought Mr Towns (St Mirren), who quickly mentioned the fact that the St Mirren had talked it over – (fancy only talked it over) – and that they thought it a very good thing, too. Loyal to the Scottish Association in the meantime, and also that it be amateur, was his parting salute. Thinking, no doubt, it would never do for St Mirren alone to embody Paisley's opinion, the Abercorn delegate, Mr Hastie, gaining confidence as he proceeded, mentioned that his club had the subject discussed on Tuesday night, but they were not prepared to submit anything definite. You will observe, gentle reader, the similarity of the speakers' sentiments. Mr Hastie proceeded to say he was not prepared to say anything officially. It was his opinion the League, if amateur, would be a welcome change, and a great aid to the match secretary. League matches would draw better, and they would have increased gates, which was much needed in these days of increased expenditure and improved grounds.

Mr Lamb had by this time got his sea legs. He is better, Mr Editor, at waving the umpire's flag than making a speech in the Council Chamber. He had nothing new to say beyond informing the meeting Mr Walker and himself were commissioned to attend and report result. It was certainly the St Bernard's desire to support the League movement, if it did not go in opposition to the existing Association, and (in a lower tone, as if he was afraid of the sound of his vocal organ) that it be strictly amateur.

The discussion was on the same lines, and the Cambuslang representative again took relief in a cigarette, at which his colleague, Mr R. Livingstone, seemed dreadfully tickled. Don't confound this latter gentlemen with the genial one of our staff, who would as soon be found blowing the big trumpet in a Salvation Army band as sitting discussing a project which had in any wise a contrary policy to the powers that be. The tobacco was contagious, and Mr Henderson lit his pipe.

Mr Lawrence again aired his views to the enlightenment of those around. The mild and discriminating nature of his remarks met with my approval. Generally speaking, he said there was a decided feeling against the proposed League taking any form of cognisance of professionalism or clashing with the SFA. The Dumbarton were strongly opposed to professionalism, which must not be encouraged in the slightest degree. If at all possible, he urged the League should be worked with the SFA as a head centre. Then its matches would clash as little as possible with Scottish Cup ties. If the League would interfere with the progress of the smaller clubs it would be a hardship, and, he considered, if this were so, they would not be justified in doing anything like that. It would be beneficial were the Association to exempt certain clubs and work at the same time, the League matches. Some arrangements could be made for this purpose. He thought the best idea would be to approach the clubs at the general meeting in May. The proposal was not a new one, for five or six years ago the representative of their club had advocated unsuccessfully before the SFA that a proportionate number of clubs be excluded from the cup competitions for a certain length of time. Now he found the present agitation was only the germination of that scheme on a much wider basis.

The remarks from the chair led to a considerable discussion on the details involved by the adoption of the scheme, and the avoidance of friction with the SFA. The representatives all expressed themselves, however, favourable to the formation of a League, and for a time lost sight of a motion, by Mr M'Laughlin, to press its adoption, in their anxiety to discuss issues. The chairman said the sentiments of some of the speakers were not his own, and urged that no alternative be put to the Association in the event of their failing to grant any proposal that might be decided at this meeting. The feeling, however, was decidedly in favour of a constituted League apart from the Association, and yet paying all due respect to its laws. Mr Mellish pointed out that, before taking any definite steps, the representatives would require to have their various committees' instructions. A small committee should be appointed to draft out the Constitution and Rules of the proposed League, and submit it to the clubs.

The Chairman again pressed that they should run parallel with the SFA. The Celtic representative asked the meeting if they imagined the Association would bear evidence, and adjudicate protests on their behalf. Were they to run the League on the line of County Jurisdiction? Mr Lawrence thought the SFA, if reasonably met, would provide some arrangement for a satisfactory method of working the League. Messrs Henderson, Smith, and M'Laughlin sustained the discussion, which now veered round to another tack. Mr Montgomery (Third Lanark) considered the term 'League' obnoxious, which brought out the retort from the Cowlairs man, amid laughter, that 'they were not leagued together for evil purposes'. Mr Montgomery thought the preferable name would be 'The Football Union'. Mr Smith increased the hilarity by stating it ought to be 'The Football Benefit Society'. The meeting was most harmonious, and eventually the following motion by Mr J. H. M'Laughlin, seconded by Mr Richardson (Heart of Midlothian), was approved of unanimously:- 'That a committee be appointed from this meeting to draft the rules and constitution of the proposed League, and submit them to the various clubs determined upon; and that these clubs be requested to send representatives with full powers to a meeting to be afterwards convened'.

The following were appointed a sub-committee to draft rules and constitution:- Messrs Henderson (Cowlairs), Lawrance (Dumbarton), Graham (Renton), Towns (St Mirren), Thomson (Third Lanark), M'Laughlin (Celtic) and Wilton (Rangers). In so far as taking a minute of the proceedings was concerned, Mr Lawrence allowed his name to stand as secretary pro. tem. Mr Mellish was proposed for convener, but declined to go on the committee. Mr M'Laughlin agreed to the duties, after some pressure. The initial resolutions to the meeting, to be moved in the name of Renton, in virtue of the prominent part that club had taken in connection with the whole affair. The clubs present pledged their united support.

The curtain falls on the first part of a drama which marks a distinct epoch in the history of Association football in Scotland. Is it the beginning of the end?

Following on from this meeting, the league became official on 30 April 1890. The first weekend of league football was to be played on 16 August 1890. However, while the clubs were excited for that opening, the press weren't so eager. The issue most of the press seemed to have was that Queen's Park, a club that had been clear from the start about their feelings towards a league and reasons for not joining, were absent. The press seemed to see the lack of Queen's Park's participation as them being usurped as Scotland's foremost footballing institution and being frozen out by these younger, less established clubs. Despite the reality being that Queen's had been invited to join the league, the outspoken *Scottish Sport* stated the following on the eve of that opening weekend: 'Our first and last objection to them [the league] is that they exist. The entire rules stink of finance, money-making and money-grabbing.'

As the press were being as positive as ever, the first weekend got underway. At this point it really should be pointed out that as much as the press weren't giving the league much backing, the league never really helped itself either. Prior to that opening weekend, one of the 12 teams, St Bernard's of Edinburgh, weren't elected to the league, and instead of trying to find a replacement, the SFL ploughed on with an odd number of teams. Fortunately, after only five matches, the number dropped to ten teams.

That opening weekend's results were:

Celtic 1 Renton 4
Cambuslang 8 Vale of Leven 2
Dumbarton 1 Cowlairs 1
Rangers 5 Heart of Midlothian 2

The opening weekend had more than just high-scoring matches. The attendances at all the matches were a lot higher than even the most optimistic person could have hoped. Over 1,000 spectators turned out at both Cambuslang and

Dumbarton, respectively. At Ibrox over 4,000 hardy souls were present, but this was nothing compared with over 10,000 folks at the original Celtic Park. After the attendance figures were released even the stone-faced *Scottish Sport* had to concede that the numbers were greatly higher than those at most friendlies and early cup rounds.

With the success of that first season, it became clear that more and more clubs were wanting to join and that sticking to being amateur was simply not possible. Most clubs were paying players by this point and this was a poorly kept secret. Finally, in 1893, under increasing pressure, the SFA backed down and professionalism was permitted in Scotland. As well as professionalism being allowed in 1893, a Second Division was added to the SFL. This would carry on until the outbreak of the First World War, when it would be suspended until 1921. The original Second Division would have no direct relegation from or promotion to the top flight but required the top teams in the second tier to be promoted through votes from the top tier. Thankfully, this system was removed in 1922, a year after the Second Division returned after the war, when automatic promotion and relegation were introduced.

A Third Division was added in 1923, but it soon became clear that it wasn't going to be economically sustainable just yet. By the midpoint of the third season in 1926, the Third Division was abandoned. After the Second World War the Third Division was tried again. In the shake-up after the war the divisions were renamed 'A', 'B' and 'C', with the 'C Division' having reserve teams in it. By 1949 the 'C Division' had been split into North East and South West. This lasted until 1955 when the reserves were pulled from the league, leaving just five 'C Division' teams. It was decided that instead of trying again it would be easier to promote the five remaining teams to the 'B Division'. So, at the start of 1956, the divisions were renamed again as the First Division and Second Division, which had 18 and 19 teams, respectively.

Things were then left alone for a comparatively long time until 1975, when in an attempt to increase attendance numbers, the SFL split again, this time into Premier, First and Second Divisions. This was done so the top teams would play each other more often and hopefully raise attendance and interest. By 1994, though, things would change again, this time to four divisions of ten teams. This only survived until 1998, when the Scottish Premier League (SPL) split from the SFL, following the example in England. With this split in 1998, the SFL dropped back to three divisions.

From 1998, things remained the same until 2013 when, finally, the SPL and SFL merged to form the Scottish Professional Football League (SPFL). With this merger the 123-year history of the SFL came to an end.

Sadly, at no point during the time of the SFL was a pyramid system introduced. This meant that unless a team resigned, went bust or were thrown out of the league, a new team couldn't join. The only method was through elections whenever an opportunity arose. This method was often expensive and difficult as the rules about what was required by the clubs would often change at short notice. With the coming of the SPFL, though, things finally changed, and since the advent of the pyramid play-offs, three teams have come into the SPFL from both the Highland and Lowland Leagues.

Scottish Football League 1890/91
First Division champions: Dumbarton and
Rangers (shared)
Relegated: Cowlairs (not re-elected)

Scottish Football League 2012/13
First Division champions: Partick Thistle
First Division relegated: Airdrie United,
Dunfermline Athletic
Second Division champions: Queen of the South
Second Division relegated: Albion Rovers
Third Division champions: Rangers

Throughout its 123-year history, over 80 teams were members of the SFL, with 11 different title winners. During this time, the league adapted on many occasions according to the times it was in and the needs of its clubs. While it made mistakes throughout its history, and even acted cold-heartedly at times, no one can say that the volunteers and committee members didn't give it their all. When the merger happened in 2013, everyone knew it was for the benefit of Scottish football, but few could say that losing this institution that had been created two centuries before in a smoke-filled room within a Glasgow hotel didn't raise even a tinge of sadness within them.

Renton

IN THE 1870s, Scotland was a hotbed of club football, and it was in 1872 that Scottish club football really took off, when of the 22 clubs formed around the world, 11 were in Scotland, ten of which were in Glasgow and Dunbartonshire.

Renton Football Club were one of those formed in 1872. Renton even now has a population of less than 3,000 people, the village sandwiched in the five-mile gap between Balloch on the banks of Loch Lomond and the former shipbuilding town of Dumbarton. Although the football club was founded in the same year as local rivals Dumbarton and Vale of Leven (in Alexandria), Renton weren't one of the eight forming the SFA in 1873. They were, though, one of the first 16 clubs to take part in the first-ever Scottish Cup.

It was at ten minutes to three on 18 October 1873 that Renton took on Kilmarnock at Crosshill in Glasgow. The team from West Dunbartonshire came out on top, 2-0. Although it has been difficult to obtain confirmation, three newspapers from the time claim that this was the first-ever competitive football match in Scotland. The *Glasgow News* of 20 October reported that: 'The Kilmarnock club were at a disadvantage through not being thoroughly conversant with association rules, having formerly played the rugby game,' and went on to say: 'The Renton side received several free kicks in succession through some of the "Auld Killies" men persistently using their hands.'

That season would see Renton get through to the last four of the cup. After beating Kilmarnock, they went on to beat local rivals Dumbarton 1-0 after a replay. However, they went out of the cup on 13 December, losing 2-0 to eventual winners Queen's Park. The following season, though, Renton did even better. This time 23 clubs entered the cup and, after receiving a walkover in the first round, Renton reached the final. After beating another local rival Helensburgh 2-0 at home, they had another home tie, this time beating Glasgow team Eastern 1-0. In the semis, though, they were taken to a replay by neighbours Dumbarton after a 1-1 draw at home. Renton won the replay 1-0 to go through to the final against Queen's Park. In the final at Hampden Park, in front of 7,000 spectators, Renton were soundly beaten 3-0.

After their cup final appearance of 1875 the club struggled to get into the latter rounds of the competition until 1885. In this same season that Queen's Park reached their second FA Cup Final, Renton won through to their second Scottish Cup Final. En route they beat Vale of Leven Wanderers (the club's second team) 2-1, then in the next round travelled to Falkirk to play East Stirlingshire, where they ran riot, winning 10-2. That scoreline, though, was only the fourth-biggest of the day. Dunfermline were beaten 11-1 by Hearts, but both of these results were nothing compared with Vale of Leven beating Campsie Central 14-0 and Yoker winning 17-0 against Tayavalla.

In the third round Renton again ran up a massive goal tally in a 9-2 victory over Glasgow team Northern, then after receiving a bye to the quarter-final, they hosted Rangers, coming out on top 5-3. In the semis they travelled to Edinburgh to play Hibernian, where they ran out winners in a tight match, 3-2, but it was enough to see them into the final.

In the final they ran out against their classic rivals Vale of Leven. After a 0-0 draw witnessed by an unlucky 2,500 people, Renton ran out 3-1 winners in the replay to lift their first Scottish Cup, in a match watched by a more respectable 5,000 fortunate souls. During their cup run Renton had scored 32 goals in seven matches.

The following season the club again made it to the final, beating Kirkintilloch Athletic 15-0 on 12 September 1885 in their first-round match. This scoreline, as impressive as it was, was absolutely nothing compared with Arbroath beating Bon Accord 36-0, and on the same day Dundee Harp put 35 goals past Aberdeen Rovers. In the second round Renton played against the short-lived team Dumbarton Athletic, winning 7-2, then in the third round squeezed past Albion 1-0 to set up a match against Cowlairs in the fourth round, which they won comfortably, 4-0. Their fifth-round tie was a repeat of the previous season's final against Vale of Leven. Again, it went to a replay. This time round the first match ended 2-2, but in the replay Renton won 3-0. After a bye into the semis, they travelled again to Edinburgh to play Hibernian in a match they won 2-0 to put them into the final against Queen's Park. However, unlike the previous season, they wouldn't walk away with the cup, beaten 3-1 in torrential rain. That season in the cup, Renton scored 35 goals in eight matches.

In 1886/87, Renton played in the English FA Cup, beating Accrington and Blackburn Rovers before finally being put out by Preston North End, 2-0 at home. They did lift the Glasgow Merchants' Charity Cup that season, though.

However, it would be season 1887/88 that would be the greatest in the club's history. Firstly, they won the Scottish Cup, scoring 35 goals in seven matches during their run, including beating Cambuslang 6-1 in the final on 4 February 1888. This, though, was just the warm-up act.

In 1888, Preston North End were one of the greatest teams in England and would the following year win the first-ever league season in England, and do it unbeaten. In the 1888 English FA Cup Final they came up against West Bromwich Albion, but were so confident about victory that before the match kicked off, they asked to have their photograph taken with the cup, because afterwards their white shirts would be muddy, which wouldn't make for such a good picture. However, as often happens when a team get cocky before a match, they were stunned by being beaten 2-1 at The Oval. After the match the Preston captain stood motionless in the centre circle for several minutes, so much so that a policeman had to tap him on the shoulder to get him to move off the pitch.

In the previous season a tentative move had been made by the clubs who had won the English and Scottish FA Cups to play a match that would become 'The Association Football

Championship of the World'. That first match was between Aston Villa and Hibernian, which ended in a 3-0 win for Villa at Perry Barr, leading them to be known as the very first 'world club champions'.

So, in 1888, after Renton won the Scottish Cup, they contacted Preston North End to organise a match between the teams, as everyone believed that Preston would win the FA Cup. However, when West Brom took the trophy, Preston simply walked away from the agreed match with Renton. So, a letter was sent to West Brom to ask whether they would take part instead. They agreed, so on 19 May 1888 at Hampden Park the two champions faced off.

The Scottish game at this time was in a stage of major crisis, with the creation of the English Football League in 1888 and the allowance of professionalism in England since 1885. These changes had led to a mass migration of Scottish players to England and had a major impact on the clubs in Scotland as they tried to keep hold of their players. It therefore forced several clubs in Scotland to start paying players secretly. This included, but wasn't limited to, Hibs, Rangers, Celtic and Hearts. These clubs had reportaedly two sets of books, one they let the SFA see and one that was actually accurate.

When in 1888 Renton lined up to face West Brom, it was seen as a battle of the old-school amateur players, who simply played for the love of the game, against a team of mercenaries, who were only there for the money. It was a dream match for the Scottish press, who had pushed the line of the English players being paid to within an inch of its life. Renton ran out 4-1 winners and became the world champions. Granted it was only between English and Scottish teams, but it was still a great accolade to have and to claim.

The 'world championship game' would only be played four times. Following the victories for Aston Villa and Renton, it wasn't played again until 1895 when Sunderland beat Hearts 5-3. Within the Sunderland team that day was Johnny Campbell, who had also played for Renton in 1888 when they won the title, therefore becoming the only player to have helped both a Scottish and English team to become world champions.

The final time the championship was played was in 1902 when Hearts won, beating Tottenham Hotspur 3-1 in a replay.

Renton built on their 1888 victory by finally getting to take on Preston North End in a match at Hampden on 2 June 1888, winning 4-1. It was after this that the club commissioned a cup to be made, which is now on display at Hampden Park, stating that Renton were indeed world champions. To drive home this fact, they also had a sign made that was hung on the pavilion at their home ground Tontine Park stating that Renton FC were, even for a small time, Champions of the World.

By 1890, clubs in Scotland were starting to become restless, having viewed the success of the league in England and wanting some of the action themselves. Renton played a major part in the founding of the SFL, including sending the notice out to other clubs to attend a meeting to create a league. They played their first league match on 16 August 1890, travelling to the original Celtic Park, where they won 4-1 in front of 10,000 fans.

Renton's time in league football was interesting to say the least, and despite their essential role in the creation of the league, it didn't stop them from being one of the first casualties of the system.

In September 1890, Adventurers complained to the SFA about a Scottish Cup tie they had lost to St Bernard's on the grounds that the opposition were paying players, after a player transfer from Dunfermline Athletic to the Edinburgh team seemed strange. During the following investigation it transpired that the player had been lured away by a job in a biscuit factory. The suspicion came from the fact that in the job he did outside of football, he was earning more in Fife than he would in Edinburgh. Soon, though, it became clear that he was receiving an extra ten shillings per football match he played in.

On 25 September 1890, the SFA found St Bernard's guilty of concealing professionalism and they were suspended. With this judgement, the club met that night and formed a new team named Edinburgh Saints. To show just how undaunted they were by the SFA, they kept the entire same playing squad and membership. The following week, the 'new' club organised a friendly with Renton. Renton attempted to secure clearance from the SFA to play the match but were told very clearly not to play it. Renton, though, on the back of a promise of good money, carried on regardless and played the match.

The SFA took a dim view, as the *Scottish Sport* wrote afterwards:

> The managers of the St. Bernard and the Renton must have been very short-sighted indeed if they

imagined that the mere change of name was sufficient to clear the club of the consequences of their peregrinations in the paths of professionalism … The sentence is a severe one, the expulsion from the Association of the two clubs, the suspension of the players involved until the end of the season, and the social annihilation of the officials concerned.

This sentence meant that Renton played only five matches of the very first season of league football in Scotland. Renton and St Bernard's were merely the example set by the SFA in its final days of fighting against professionalism. When the league had been created it had allowed players to be paid a fee for expenses. Shockingly, in an unforeseen move, the bigger clubs started paying players higher expenses but maintained that they weren't paying players to play, just to travel. Finally, in 1890, the SFA took a deep look into clubs' finances after the St Bernard's affair.

As this investigation started, a sense of panic ran through almost all Scottish clubs, none more so than Hibs, Celtic, Rangers and the unfortunate Cowlairs. Firstly, Hibs had some interesting things in their books. To start with, the SFA asked all clubs to show them the last five years' worth of accountancy books. In 1887, Hibs had won the Scottish Cup, defeating Dumbarton in the final. Although a private detective had found out that a Hibs player, William Groves, was being paid by the club four times what he earned as an apprentice stonemason for 'broken time' to allow him to play football, the SFA still rejected Dumbarton's protest about Hibs paying players. However, justice would come shortly after when in the weeks after the cup final the Hibs treasurer, a Mr McFadden, disappeared to Canada with most of the club's funds and even some money belonging to the Archdiocese of Edinburgh.

The extent of the investigation the SFA launched can be questioned as Hibs had three different treasurers in that five-year period. Yet somehow all five sets of books came in with the same handwriting on them. Rangers, on the other hand, had somehow lost the safe keys so would need to wait for the safe to be opened and, strangely, when the safe was opened two of the sets of books were badly burned. Celtic, though, had arguably the best reason. Their books were a week late being sent to the SFA, which Celtic said was because the people in the secretary's house had all come down with a fever, so the books needed to be disinfected. They had sent the books away to the Glasgow sanitary authorities to be cleaned before sending them on to the SFA. Even with these interesting stories, every club but Cowlairs passed the SFA checks and were allowed to carry on as before.

Renton, though, were, for now at least, banned from all footballing activity. So, the club, not wanting to take this ruling lying down, decided to take the SFA to court. They claimed £5,000 against the SFA on the grounds of lost earnings because engagements were being cancelled, the vested interest in their fame as a club (even in the court papers they mentioned being world champions) and the fact they had brought their ground up to the new requirements the SFA had set out. The club took the SFA to the Court of Session in Edinburgh, where they argued that friendlies shouldn't impact on them in league competition as long as league matches weren't moved for them. Renton managed to win their fight, were awarded the £5,000 plus expenses and were restored to the SFA. From the 1891/92 season, they were back in the league.

By 1893 professionalism was finally permitted in Scottish football, and while this was good news for most, Renton were starting to struggle. By the end of the 1893/94 season they were relegated to the Second Division. The club was small in size and even in their heyday could only attract crowds of around 300 people, so now they started to come under extreme financial pressure. During the amateur years, clubs were only paying for travel costs, which prior to the league campaign wasn't so bad, but as soon as you add wages and stadium requirements, 300 spectators aren't going to bring a great deal of income.

The 1894/95 season was a mixed bag for Renton. In the league they struggled to pay for travel to away matches, and in their last match of the season they played a much-needed monied glamour friendly against Queen's Park instead of travelling to Dundee to play Dundee Wanderers. While their league form was terrible, Renton did manage to get through to what would be their last Scottish Cup Final. They played none other than St Bernard's at Ibrox Park, where the Edinburgh team ran out 2-1 winners.

Despite this cup final appearance, Renton's time in the top leagues was drawing to a close. In 1895/96 they finished third in the second tier and then sixth the following season. It was, however, in 1897/98 that they finally pulled out of the league, after just four matches of the season. The club that had helped form a league, whose committee had taken the first initial steps into creating that league – a club who had been world champions less than ten years previously – played their final SFL match in September 1897 in a 3-1 home defeat to Leith Athletic.

Since they had played that friendly against Edinburgh Saints in 1890, Renton had been on a downward spiral. Whereas the other teams in the league had become used to the format and the requirements of league football, Renton had been somewhat more cavalier in their approach to league matches and kept getting their knuckles rapped for opting to play lucrative friendlies instead of their league fixtures.

After 1897, Renton dropped into the Western League, where local rivals Vale of Leven were also playing. Meanwhile, Hamilton Academical took Renton's place in the SFL. However, Renton would go on to play in the Scottish Cup until the club's very end. They did manage to have one last cup run in 1907, which included beating Dundee, who would go on to finish second in the top flight that season, and facing St Bernard's, who were by now leading the Second Division, before being knocked out by Queen's Park.

The former football world champions would drift on until finally folding in 1922. They had entered the 1922/23 Scottish Cup but failed to turn up for the tie and subsequently folded. The club's ground was sold and used for housing. The former centre circle is now a memorial garden to the club from a tiny village in Scotland that was once the greatest team in the world.

The story of Renton Football Club deserves to be known more widely than it is, as they were undisputed champions of the world, even if it was for a short period of time. Sadly, no club was ever formed in the town in the aftermath of the team folding. If you ever wish to see the ground where the world champions once played, it can be found just off John Street in Renton.

In 1988 there was a match played between Dumbarton and West Bromwich Albion. The match had been agreed many years before and should have been between Renton and West Brom. However, as Renton had become defunct, the nearest senior team left from the area was Dumbarton. In the match, West Brom lost again, 2-1 this time, which led to the local paper in West Bromwich running the headline 'Second World Cup Defeat for Albion!'

Vale of Leven

THE VALE of Leven Football Club was formed in 1872, in the small milling town of Alexandria just to the south of Loch Lomond and hugging the River Leven. The town today is quiet and viewed by most people as a commuter town for Glasgow. Alexandria is the biggest of the townships that make up the Vale of Leven (Balloch, Bonhill, Jamestown, Renton and Alexandria) but it's a young town compared with the rest. It was for most of its history just a fork in the road with an inn and a ferry crossing the river. The original fork can still be viewed if you go to the fountain on the town's main street.

The reason why Alexandria became the biggest town in the Vale of Leven is simple. If you were to visit the area, once you leave Dumbarton you will see that on the east bank of the River Leven there is just a small bit of flat land that rises into hills very quickly; therefore, the towns of Bonhill and Jamestown were limited in growth capacity. At the north of the river is the town of Balloch, but this too is squashed in between hills and Loch Lomond. On the west side of the river there is a much longer plateau; however, the town of Renton is situated just at the edge of the hills before Dumbarton, so is again limited on space. Alexandria, on the other hand, is situated on a nice, broad, flat piece of land, which made expanding as a town much easier. This and the fact that the landowner owned almost all the land in the Vale of Leven helped the town of Alexandria grow.

Prior to 1800 the local economy consisted of people working for the local landlords, farming, coal mining or on the riverbanks doing tanning. As a result, the population was low. After 1800, though, things took a turn with the clearances in the Highlands and the Industrial Revolution taking shape. A local landowner built a small cotton mill in Alexandria and soon the people followed. This was enhanced when in 1850 the Caledonian & Dumbarton Junction Railway opened a line through to Balloch. By 1858 the town was connected to the national railway network and soon the factories in the area could easily bring in more raw materials and transport products out again, much quicker than ever before.

With its development happening as quickly as it did, the town, which at the start of the 19th century had a population of about 200, soon expanded to nearly 6,000 people by 1870. This increase plus the ease of getting in and out of Glasgow meant that news, sport and people travelled more quickly than ever before. So, as news was travelling fast, it wasn't long before Queen's Park FC (the prominent club of the time) heard rumours that a group of shinty players from the town wanted to try their hand at playing rugby. With this news, Queen's made contact and offered to show them how to play football instead. So, in the summer of 1872, Queen's travelled to Alexandria to play them, and after the match the shinty players seemed so impressed with the new sport that they formed a club on 20 August 1872, calling themselves the Vale of Leven Rugby and Athletic Club.

Soon after the club was founded they changed the name to Vale of Leven Football and Athletic Club, and by December 1872 they travelled to the south side of Glasgow to face Queen's Park at Hampden, where they were soundly beaten 3-0. A few weeks later, though, they faced Queen's again, this time in Alexandria, and they held the giants of the time to a 0-0 draw. This might not seem much of a feat, but at a time when Queen's Park were rolling three, four and five nils past everyone, to stop their potent attack was quite an achievement.

On 13 March 1873 Vale of Leven were present at, and one of the founding clubs of, the SFA and the Scottish Cup. They entered the competition that first year, but things wouldn't go to plan. The club had grown in popularity and local professional runners James White and John Ferguson had started to play for the team. Ferguson was a phenomenal athlete who once ran a mile-long race in four minutes, 18 seconds, which even by modern-day standards is a very respectable time.

With the players the club was attracting starting to raise a few eyebrows, they entered the 1873/74 Scottish Cup, where they were drawn to face local rivals Dumbarton. However, with Vale of Leven's best player John Ferguson being a professional athlete, Dumbarton protested to the SFA that the match shouldn't be played as professionalism was banned in football. The SFA agreed with Dumbarton and they were handed a walkover into the second round. Vale protested that it was somewhat ridiculous that they were being punished for having a professional sportsman in their ranks when the sport in which he was a professional was running and not football. They argued that other clubs had people who were professional in other fields outside football, so should they be banned? While the argument was understandable, it wasn't unsurprising to find out that the protest was dismissed, and Vale didn't get to play in the first Scottish Cup.

The following season's Scottish Cup seemed to be going better when Vale took on Clydesdale in October 1874. They drew 0-0 but before the replay they withdrew when it became clear that Clydesdale were in the process of protesting the result because, yet again, John Ferguson had played and, yet again, it seemed that the SFA were about to take Clydesdale's side in the fight.

Finally, in 1875/76 Vale managed to play a cup tie without anyone protesting. They received a walkover in the first round, then on 13 November 1875 achieved their first-ever win in the cup, beating local rivals Renton 3-0. This, and a following-round win over Mauchline, 6-0, took them to the quarter-final against Queen's Park. Their opponents were still at the top of the game, although their power was somewhat beginning to wane, but in a tightly fought contest Queen's prevailed 2-1.

In the next season's cup, though, things were much better for Vale. After ploughing through the first few rounds, beating Helensburgh and Vale of Leven Rovers with remarkable ease, they faced up to Third Lanark, the previous season's runners-up. In front of 4,000 spectators, Vale edged past Thirds 1-0 to go through. For the next round they were drawn against

Busby, and after squashing them 4-0 they were through to a quarter-final against the undefeated Queen's Park. With two goals from John Baird, Vale came from behind to beat Queen's 2-1, a monumental achievement that didn't go unnoticed at the time, with papers in both Scotland and the UK as a whole carrying the story. After defeating Queen's, Vale carried on, and after beating Ayr Thistle resoundingly 9-0 in the semi-final were finally through to the Scottish Cup Final, where they came up against Glasgow Rangers.

The final of the 1877 Scottish Cup was played out over more minutes than any other. The first attempt to play the final was on 17 March 1877 at the West of Scotland Cricket Club in Partick, where after 90 minutes the score sat at 1-1. Vale had taken the lead early in the second half, only for Rangers to equalise five minutes later and the match ended in a stalemate. In the second attempt, played at the same ground on 7 April, the score ended 1-1 again. This time round Rangers took the lead after seven minutes, but just after the break Vale equalised after a stramash in the box. At the end of 90 minutes the two teams agreed to play extra time (the first time this had ever been done in Scotland). Towards the end of the extra period a shot was cannoned in that hit the underside of the bar and bounced out. The Rangers players were screaming for the goal, and while the referee and linesman were talking, the Rangers fans ran on to the pitch claiming it too. Once it became clear that the fans wouldn't be moved it was decided that no goal should be awarded to Rangers. So, with the Rangers players protesting that their own fans had cost them their first-ever cup success, the tie went to another replay, this time on Friday, 13 April

1877, to be played at the slightly safer ground of Hampden Park. Again, it was an end-to-end affair, but with the score at 2-2 and looking like extra time was again going to be needed, Bob Paton popped up in the 89th minute to slot in the winner to make it 3-2 to the Vale and end a fantastic season in style.

Vale retained the Scottish Cup in 1877/78 by beating Third Lanark 1-0 in a dull affair in front of just 5,000 spectators at Hampden Park. After this second cup victory they went on to face the English FA Cup winners Wanderers at The Oval in London, beating them 3-1 in a match that showed just how good the Scottish passing game could be.

In the following season Vale matched Queen's Park's record of winning the Scottish Cup three times in a row. The final was played against Rangers and ended in a 1-1 draw; however, Rangers claimed that a goal had been scored but the referee said the ball never crossed the line. Rangers then lodged a protest with the SFA, who also dismissed the claim. So, when the final was replayed a week later, Rangers refused to attend and, as a result, Vale kicked off, scored a goal and were awarded the tie and cup by the SFA for their hat-trick of trophy victories.

Over the next few seasons, Vale had a mixed bag of results in the Scottish Cup, with a first-round loss to Dumbarton in 1879/80 before a run to the semi-final in 1880/81, followed by early-round exits in the next couple of seasons. Finally, 1882/83 saw them reach the final again, this time to face off against local rivals Dumbarton. The match on 31 March 1883 saw the Vale come back from 2-0 down to draw 2-2. A week later in front of 8,000 spectators, Dumbarton again took a 2-0 lead, before Vale pulled one back ten minutes from time to create a nervy ending. However, Dumbarton held on throughout the final few minutes to win their only-ever Scottish Cup.

Vale matched their previous achievements in the Scottish Cup by getting to another final; however, this time they came up against the dominant Queen's Park. The Vale team, though, were facing major issues with players being unavailable for a variety of reasons, so they approached Queen's Park in the hope of delaying the final. With Queen's Park indifferent to the idea of moving the date of the final, Vale then approached the SFA but they refused to move it. As a result, Vale refused to attend the final so Queen's Park were awarded a walkover.

In 1884/85 Vale made it through to yet another Scottish Cup Final against a different local rival, this time Renton. The final went to a replay after a bore draw at Hampden on 21 February 1885. In the replay a week later Renton ran out easy winners, 3-1, in front of 5,000 people.

For the rest of the 1880s Vale struggled to get to the later stages of the cup. However, after a few seasons of doing relatively poorly in the competition, they again reached the final in 1889/90, against Queen's Park in a match played at Ibrox. Just after half an hour the Vale took the lead and held it until the 89th minute when Queen's equalised through James Hamilton, taking the final to another replay. A week later at Ibrox in front of 13,000 spectators Vale again took a first-half lead and held it until the final ten minutes, when Queen's scored two in two minutes to take the lead. Having been dealt that body blow, Vale didn't recover and ended up losing the final for the fourth time.

With their success in the Scottish Cup, having won it three times and been in the final seven times, it was no surprise that Vale of Leven were invited to the meeting that created the SFL in 1890, with them voting in favour of the league being created.

Vale played their first league match on 16 August 1890 against Cambuslang, being beaten 5-0. This opening defeat was a sign of what was to come, with the club managing just five victories all season and finishing in ninth place, thus facing the uncertainty of a re-election vote. They were challenged by non-league clubs for their league position but, fortunately, they survived the vote.

The season that followed was one of the worst ever recorded in Scotland. Vale of Leven played 22 matched in which they conceded 100 goals and didn't win all season, a record that stood for 126 years until 2017/18 when Brechin City went through the entire Championship season without winning a match. As Vale finished bottom of the league, they faced another re-election vote. However, things were made more complicated as the league announced that the numbers would drop from 12 to 10 teams. This meant that Vale would be fighting three other current league teams, as well as four non-league teams for one position.

Unsurprisingly, Vale were voted out of the SFL and entered the Scottish Football Alliance for the 1892/93 season. Despite a respectable eighth-place finish, they left the Alliance after just one season, given that they had a sizeable debt and the crowd numbers for league matches weren't as high as for Scottish Cup ties. Between 1893 and 1902 Vale of Leven played the occasional Scottish Cup tie and friendlies but didn't re-join any form of league until the summer of 1902, when they entered the Scottish Football Combination.

In the summer of 1905, the SFL extended the Second Division and opened it up to four teams to gain membership to the league. Vale of Leven applied to regain membership of the SFL, and while they had performed respectably in the Combination, they had hardly put in top performances, so it was a surprise that they were successful in the voting for the league positions.

Vale of Leven re-entered the SFL for the 1905/06 season and, given that their performances in the Combination hadn't been fantastic, it was little surprise that they finished in 11th place and faced another re-election vote. They survived this one and then pushed on to achieve a wonderful second-place finish in the 1906/07 season. This meant that, this time, Vale entered the election at the end of the season to gain promotion to the First Division; not surprisingly they weren't successful.

Vale of Leven had a drop-off the following season after the failed vote for the top flight, ending the season in tenth spot. This, though, was just a blip, as in 1908/09 they put together a real fight for the title, right up until the penultimate weekend of the season when a 1-1 draw was enough to see them fall out of the title race. They finished in third place and didn't enter the vote for the top flight. The 1909/10 season saw Vale start off fantastically, but after the turn of the year their form dropped and saw them fall to sixth place.

In the five seasons leading up to the First World War, Vale finished in the bottom two on four occasions, managing to survive three re-election votes. However, after finishing bottom in 1914/15, they avoided the re-election vote altogether when the SFL suspended the Second Division for the remainder of the war.

Due to this suspension, in 1915 Vale entered the Western League along with most of the other teams from the west coast within the second tier. Surprisingly for Vale, they won the Western League in 1915/16 and remained in that league until 1921 when the Second Division returned and they re-entered the league system.

Vale's time in the Western League had been a sort of renaissance for them, winning the title once and having consistently high league finishes. They then carried this form into their return to the SFL and finished the first season in fourth place, only three points from second, although they were 16 points from promotion.

The form Vale showed in that first season wasn't repeated in the second, as they slipped down the league and finished in 18th place, just two points above the re-election spots at the bottom of the table. Then, in the summer of 1923, the SFL took the decision to introduce a new Third Division with automatic promotion and relegation to the Second Division, meaning teams in the bottom two would be relegated to the third tier for the first time instead of facing a re-election vote.

In 1923/24, Vale's form didn't improve and they ended up 19th, in the relegation places, just one point from safety. As they prepared for their first season in the third tier, they became early favourites to go straight back up. A 4-1 away win over Helensburgh gave the impression that they would be in for a good season, and this proved to be correct as they went on to achieve nine wins in a row. However, issues were starting to occur off the park, as the club was warned and fined twice for reducing admission prices below the league's set minimum price.

As the season went on, Vale were locked in a tight promotion battle along with Nithsdale Wanderers, Queen of the South and Solway Star. By the beginning of March, Vale were one point clear in second place and favourites, alongside Nithsdale Wanderers, for promotion, but with six matches to go Vale lost form and slipped down to fourth, finishing two points outside the promotion places.

The 1925/26 season was the final one for the Third Division and for Vale of Leven. As the season wore on many clubs were beginning to struggle to keep up with the league's guarantee of £15 to the visiting teams in every match. Most paid late and Vale were no exception to this. By April they were in serious financial trouble, with an £800 overdraft from building works at the ground compounding issues. Finally, in late April, the Vale of Leven players went on strike after the club failed to pay their wages. To add to the misery, the club were being chased by the league as they weren't able to pay match guarantees to many of the other clubs. Eventually, as Vale were one of many clubs on the brink of financial collapse, the SFL took the decision to shut the league down.

When this happened, Vale of Leven joined the Scottish Football Alliance for one season, before leaving and becoming founding members of the Provincial League, which was itself abandoned after just one season. Finally, Vale moved into a more local league but again after just one season they pulled out.

The club's finances had been taking hit after hit, and after leaving the SFL, match gates had plummeted to an average of less than 200 people. This, plus the overdraft being still maxed out, made it impossible for the club to continue. By 1929, they didn't look likely to have a future outside of the local leagues, and with the global downturn their committee took the difficult decision to fold the three-time Scottish Cup winners, 50 years after their last cup triumph.

Vale of Leven's home ground of Millburn Park continued to be used as a football ground when Vale OCOBA (Old Church Old Boys Association) used it until 1939, when they were invited to join the Scottish Football Alliance. Vale OCOBA promptly joined but as a re-formed Vale of Leven. They joined the junior ranks after the Second World War and went on to become successful, including winning the Scottish Junior Cup in 1953. They still play at Millburn Park and in 2020 joined the senior ranks as a part of the West of Scotland League.

Third Lanark

THE STORY of Third Lanark is as complicated as it is long. Unlike most of the clubs within this book, Third Lanark survived the opening exchanges of the league. They also survived the First and Second World Wars and the Great Depression, collapsing merely weeks after Celtic had become the first British team to lift the European Cup.

Season 1966/67 was arguably the best in Scottish footballing history. Scotland beat world champions England in their first international since that final, 3-2 at Wembley. In Europe, Scottish clubs were doing phenomenally. Dunfermline Athletic went out in the second round of the Inter-Cities Fairs Cup to eventual winners Dinamo Zagreb. In the same competition, Dundee United beat holders Barcelona home and away before going out in the second round to Italian giants Juventus, while Kilmarnock made it to the semi-finals before losing out to Leeds United. The Old Firm teams did even better, with Rangers making it to the final of the Cup Winners' Cup, losing in extra time, 1-0 to Bayern Munich. Meanwhile, Celtic, in spectacular fashion, got to the European Cup Final and, in a famous story, beat

Inter Milan 2-1 in Lisbon to become the first team from northern Europe to lift the trophy.

It was against this backdrop, less than a fortnight after Billy McNeill lifted that famous cup above his head, that a team playing its football less than two miles from both Celtic Park and Ibrox, in a stadium that could hold upwards of 50,000 fans, was issued a winding-up order and appointed an official liquidator by a judge at the Court of Session in Edinburgh. With the drop of that gavel the judge hammered the final nail into the coffin of a club that was 16 years older than Celtic.

As previously mentioned, the first-ever international football match took place in Glasgow on 30 November 1872. In the 4,000 crowd that day were several soldiers from the Third Lanarkshire Rifle Volunteers. Inspired by the football they had witnessed, the soldiers formally founded Third Lanark AC on 12 December 1872. A few of the founding members – Billy Dickson, Billy MacKinnon and Joseph Taylor – had played in the international and at the time as players for Queen's Park.

At a meeting soon after the founding, it was decided that Third Lanark's kit should be: 'A cowl – one end blue, the other yellow, a scarlet guernsey. Blue trousers or knickerbockers with blue stockings.' Later, it was agreed that all guernseys would have the number 3 on the front. They started off training at an old drill field, which is now the site of a primary school on Victoria Road, then shortly afterwards moved to Cathkin Park (today Govanhill Park). In 1883 they joined the newly formed Glasgow Football Association and in 1890 became a founding member of the SFL.

In 1889 Third Lanark won their first Scottish Cup but it wasn't easy to get hold of the trophy. This cup final would become known as the 'snow final'. On Saturday, 2 February 1889 the snow and wind had been building up for several days, so by the time kick-off came around the snow was ankle-deep on the pitch. However, the matchday officials stated that the pitch was still playable, and despite the players on both sides lodging protests, it went ahead. The players all agreed that, as the pitch was so bad, the match should be treated as a friendly, and they came out throwing snowballs at each other. As the match started, Celtic looked the better team, but after 20 minutes of the second half Thirds went one up. They then looked and played better and soon were two up, and wrapped the match up a minute before time with their third and final goal for 3-0. Despite the terrible conditions and the match being in doubt most of the day, it still attracted over 18,000 fans, which was a record attendance for a Scottish match at the time.

Two days later, though, at a special meeting of the SFA, the result was in question as both teams had agreed prior to the match that it should be played as a friendly. Even a signed document by both clubs wasn't enough to convince some in attendance that the result shouldn't stand. It was only after the referee was questioned on the state of the pitch that it was concluded that the match should be replayed.

The following Saturday, 9 February, the teams walked out on to the Hampden turf again. This time it was a clear day but an incredibly hard pitch. Prior to kick-off, Third Lanark lodged a protest at having to play the match again as they had won the previous one but their protest fell on deaf ears. As they kicked off the two teams were very evenly matched, but Thirds were given a helping hand when one Celtic player had to retire from the match in a time before substitutions. Celtic had to play nearly an hour with ten men. Not long after this advantage, Thirds went one up and it stayed that way until the hour mark when Celtic equalised. But late in the match Thirds scored again and took the cup home, 2-1.

Prior to 1903, Thirds had slowly been drifting from their military founding fathers. They kept their name but finally in 1903 cut their final connections with the military. That season was a massive one for the club, not only because they became a completely independent organisation, but they also moved into the second Hampden Park, quickly renamed New Cathkin Park, which would be their home for the next 64 years. On the pitch, it was a season where they won their only Scottish league championship title. In the 26 matches played they won 20 and lost only three, winning the league by four points, and in doing so cementing their place in history.

The success of those early 20th century years reached its pinnacle when in 1905 Thirds won their final piece of major silverware when they beat Rangers after a replay in the Scottish Cup. This time it was a lot simpler than their first cup success. In a match in front of 54,000 spectators, the final ended 0-0, then a week later Thirds walked away with the trophy, beating their opponents 3-1 in front of 30,000 spectators. After their second cup victory, Third Lanark held on to their position in the top pyramid in Scotland but never really challenged again. In fact, by the time war was declared on 4 August 1914, their slide down the leagues had already begun.

After the war and in the boom of the early 1920s, many teams in Scotland started to take on pre-season tours to North America, South America and Africa. Having already toured in Spain and Portugal in 1914 and the USA and Canada in 1921, Third Lanark went on a pre-season tour to South America in 1923. However, this tour was a bit different as they would play eight matches against teams in Argentina and Uruguay, including one against the Argentinian national team. The trip to Argentina was a great success and in time would prove beneficial for two reasons: firstly, when Thirds fell upon hard times in the future, the Argentinian FA sent the team equipment and kits to play in; and secondly, there was the strange story of Raith Rovers becoming shipwrecked in the Canary Islands. On the route back from Argentina, the ship Third's travelled on docked in Las Palmas to refuel during the 8,000-mile journey. As they docked they found the shipwrecked Raith Rovers team waiting for them after their own vessel had run aground.

In 1924/25, Thirds were relegated at the end of the season, which started a decade of yo-yoing between the top two divisions. It wouldn't be until the mid-1930s that they would stabilise in the top division again. This period also included their final appearance in a Scottish Cup Final in 1936, when nearly 90,000 people squeezed into Hampden Park to watch Thirds lose a closely fought match against Rangers, 1-0.

The 1930s ended with two players from the club being called up to the national team's tour of the USA in 1939, but, as in 1914, Thirds' chances of building on this success was again interrupted by war. Much like after the First World War, not much happened to the club once hostilities were over. This was until 6 November 1949 in a 4-2 defeat at home to Stirling Albion, when a young player who would later lead Scotland to a World Cup made his professional debut for the club: Ally MacLeod. Despite not really pulling up any trees in his first match, it did go down in history. As the two teams were leaving the field of play, the main stand was ablaze and the players had to rush in to grab their belongings and get out as four fire engines arrived at the ground to get the blaze under control.

It was around this time that a new man came to the club who would have a massive impact: Bill Hiddleston. He was a wholesale glass merchant and businessman who started off in the stands watching matches with his father, but in 1954 he became a member of the club's board. This, however, wouldn't last very long as he soon started to act without the knowledge of the rest of the board. The final straw came in the summer of 1955 when he spent £500 on a player without the board's permission, which led to him being removed from the board and having to pay the £500 out of his own pocket. Even after this, though, he would be back.

In January 1956, local boy and supporter Ally MacLeod was reluctantly sold to St Mirren for £8,000 in a deal he didn't want to be part of. However, he did go when told that the money was desperately needed for the club's survival. Then in 1957, Thirds appointed a manager who would lay the groundwork for the team to move forward towards their last real success. This was Bob Shankly, the older brother of Liverpool's legendary manager Bill.

However, Bob left in 1959 to take the reins at Dundee, who he would lead to a Scottish league championship and into the semi-finals in Europe, before being beaten by AC Milan. George Young took over, and the former Rangers defender took the part-time team to the Scottish League Cup Final against Hearts and to a third-place finish in the league that season. Although in the cup final Thirds played well and took the lead, they were beaten 2-1 by a Hearts team that would go on to win the league and League Cup double that season.

At the time it seemed to the outside world that Third Lanark may well be on the up again. However, this would all change at the AGM in December 1962, when it was announced that a new man had taken over as a majority shareholder of the club. Bill Hiddleston had returned and his appointment had the effect of seeing the entire management and backroom staff resign on the spot. Added to this, most of the board left at the same time, and as one director said when leaving the club for the final time, 'Good luck to Thirds and God help them.'

Thirds' decline was almost instant. At the end of 1963/64, they sold or released 23 players. The following season they finished bottom of the top tier with a mere seven points from 34 matches. There soon came even more financial problems and the players had issues getting their wages paid and often there was no hot water or power for them during training. A major contributor to the money problems was European football. In the past the Glasgow Cup had been played between Queen's Park, Third Lanark, Clyde, Partick Thistle, Celtic and Rangers, and all involved put out strong teams for the trophy. Also, it meant for the committees of the clubs that, no matter what, they would get an extra money-spinning home tie against Rangers or Celtic per season. However, once the Old Firm duo got into European competitions, they started to play their reserve teams in the Glasgow Cup and the number of fans turning out for these matches dropped massively. This meant that where once the other clubs would make a pretty penny, it was turning more often than not into a financial inconvenience to play them.

The fans had also become disillusioned by the state Third Lanark had got into, and believing that the owner of the club was out to fill his own pockets, they stopped attending. In 1959/60, 550,000 people had attended Thirds' matches, but by 1966/67 this was down to only 55,000. This was compounded when in January 1966 it was front-page news in Glasgow that the board of Third Lanark was looking at moving the club to one of the new towns that surrounded Glasgow. This news that they wanted to move and sell the land the current ground was on for housing was the moment people fully turned. Into what was to be the last season for Thirds, rumours were rife that the players had their wages supplemented with coins from the turnstiles, that they had to make their own way to away matches and that teams visiting New Cathkin Park were being asked to bring light bulbs and footballs with them.

Unbeknown to the supporters who turned up on Tuesday, 25 April 1967, they would witness the final-ever home match of Third Lanark AC in a 3-3 draw with Queen of the South. The attendance that day was a mere 325, the second-lowest attendance they ever recorded, the lowest being ten days prior when just 297 people arrived to watch them play Clydebank (the same day as the England 2 Scotland 3 fixture at Wembley).

The final-ever match for Thirds was a humiliating 5-1 defeat to Dumbarton at Boghead. That match had 581 spectators witnessing a piece of history. No one within the ground that fateful day knew that they had just watched the last-ever match in Third Lanark's history and their final-ever goalscorer in Drew Busby, who would later go on to become a hero at both Airdrie and Hearts. The team that day was Bob Russell, Tony Connell, Gerry Heaney, Hugh McLaughlan, Jim Little, Gordon McEwan, Hugh Rundall, Bobby Craig, Drew Busby, Don May and John Kinnaird. Their manager was former Rangers captain Bobby Shearer, assisted by former Scotland international John McKenzie.

It was a few weeks later that the board of Third Lanark announced that they had negotiated the sale of New Cathkin Park to the Glasgow Corporation for housing, and a new stadium for Thirds would be built in Bishopbriggs (needless to say this stadium was never built). It was in the middle of May 1967 that the board of trade launched its investigation into the club's books. A report published in October 1968 revealed that constant player squabbles and internal power struggles had been rife. Corruption was clear as well as defrauding the fans from the club lottery, which should have been a £200 prize that was rarely paid out. Added to this, it also showed that Bill Hiddleston had made every appointment personally, therefore making the people who weren't close to him more likely to leave the club and turning it from a committee of individuals into a sort of closed shop mafia.

All of these issues took their final toll when, on 7 June 1967, at the Court of Session in Edinburgh, Lord Fraser issued a winding-up order on the club and appointed an official liquidator. The court action was brought by a building company, which in 1963 had carried out work on the main stand. When the liquidator came in it was shown that club debts were higher than the value of the club by some £40,000.

On 26 June 1967, it was announced that Third Lanark AC's membership of the SFL, the league it helped to form, had been revoked. On that day, all their players were made free for transfer and the club ceased its existence.

As for the ground, which was the club's only real asset, it hosted its final football match on 13 May 1967 in the Glasgow Challenge Cup Final between Cambuslang Rangers and Rutherglen Glencairn, which ended 2-0 to Cambuslang. The ground was sold shortly afterwards to the Glasgow Corporation for £10,000 in a sale that was forced through by the Royal Bank of Scotland to pay off the overdraft. Houses would never be built on the site as Glasgow City Council blocked the sale of the land, so it remained a derelict site until 1977 when Glasgow City Parks Department paid £350,000 to convert it into an open park, which it remains to this day. If you are ever in Glasgow you can visit the site and see three of the banks of terracing that include the crush barriers.

As for the club itself, after the board of trade concluded its investigation, it was found that four of the directors had breached the Companies Act 1948 and were fined £100 each. The investigation also accused Bill Hiddleston of blatant corruption and found that 'the circumstances merited police inquiry'. However, he was never brought to justice or even questioned on his actions as, in November 1967, he died of a heart attack at a hotel in Blackpool.

Bill Hiddleston was a man who from the outside appears to have just run the club into the ground for his own benefit. History will always see this man as a crook. However, to provide some balance, he did sanction the building of a new grandstand in 1963, which, in hindsight, would be the reason a company took the club to court for non-payment of the work. He was also at the time a board member of the SFA, so to say he wasn't a football man would be somewhat unfair. With this additional knowledge, he doesn't seem like a classic asset-stripper, although his actions as owner are without doubt the reason the club, which had such a history and a collection of silverware, is no longer with us.

As for the fans who were loyal to the end, most ended up supporting another local club, many going the short distance to Queen's Park, Clyde or Pollok. Very few would go to the Old Firm duo. Unlike a lot of Scottish clubs that went into liquidation at the time, before and since, there was never a rush to re-form the club. It's argued that this is because of the way the club ended. It was such a painful decline that when they were finally laid to rest, it was mostly felt that it was for the best.

The Third Lanark name was eventually brought back to life in the 1990s, and in 2008 it was announced that they intended to get the team back to the Scottish senior leagues. Currently, they play in the Central Scottish Amateur League and they are also in negotiations with Glasgow City Council, who currently own New Cathkin Park, about playing their home matches back at the park. Should you want to visit New Cathkin Park, it's now a Glasgow city park, called Cathkin Park.

Arthurlie

BARRHEAD IS known today as an upmarket commuter town just to the south of Glasgow and Paisley. It is, in comparison with many other towns in Scotland, quite young, only being formed as a town in the late 19th century during its boom time as a centre of industry, including the Armitage Shanks porcelainware works, a tannery, an iron foundry and many coal mines in the local vicinity.

Arthurlie itself is an area within Barrhead that was one of the original four villages coming together to form the town. It was home to a mine, a cotton mill and a printworks, which gave the area a sense of local pride. It was no surprise when, during the early years of Scottish football, a club was created by the workers from these industries. In its first season, 1874, Arthurlie Football Club entered the Scottish Cup, losing 3-0 to Dumbarton.

Arthurlie spent the rest of that decade playing in the Scottish Cup and other local cup competitions, and helped to form the Renfrewshire Football Association and the subsequent Renfrewshire Cup. While in the Scottish Cup, they struggled to get past the third round, achieving some good and bad results, notably an 8-3 win against Morton and a 7-0 defeat at the hands of Queen's Park.

As the 1870s turned into the 1880s, Arthurlie's fortunes began to improve and they had a respectable run of three Scottish Cup quarter-finals in a row. In 1880/81 they were knocked out by Vale of Leven 2-0 on Christmas Day, in a match where the crowd seemingly lacked festive spirit as the subsequent report stated that they indulged 'in rounds of profane, disgusting language'. The report went on to say that this behaviour should be discouraged.

Their 1881/82 cup run was brought to an end by Kilmarnock Athletic, 5-1, who also beat them the following season, this time after a third replay. The teams faced off originally on 30 December 1882, ending in a 1-1 draw. The first replay on 3 February 1883 ended in an Arthurlie victory, 2-1, but Kilmarnock successfully appealed based on the inclusion of an ineligible player. A week later they played out another 1-1 draw, taking them to a third replay. On 17 February, nearly two months after their first match they faced each other again and, finally, Kilmarnock won 1-0 at the very death of the match to end the duel.

After their run of three quarter-finals in three years, Arthurlie struggled for the rest of the decade, making it to the fifth round only once but for the rest of the time unable to get past the early rounds of the competition. Following on from the allowance of professionalism in England, Arthurlie started to really struggle to retain its better players, partly due to the connections between the town of Stoke-on-Trent and Barrhead. This came through the Armitage Shanks works, which was headquartered in Stoke, so a lot of the better players who worked in the factory in Barrhead would strangely be offered the same job in Stoke and would start turning out for Stoke as a professional within weeks of travelling south.

By the late 1880s, Arthurlie had slipped down the pecking order and ended up not being invited as one of the clubs to take part in the meeting to create the SFL. They watched the SFL's success after that first season and instead joined with several other uninvited clubs to create the Scottish Football Federation. They then quickly proved to be the team to beat in the Federation, winning the title that first season. In the second season they slipped down to third; however, this didn't matter as the Federation was broken up when the SFL announced that it was creating a Second Division, which was to be made up of most of the clubs from the rival Scottish Football Alliance. With the Alliance losing most of its clubs to the SFL, it turned to those in the less-monied Federation to boost its numbers and all the clubs moved over, abandoning the Federation.

Arthurlie remained in the Scottish Football Alliance until 1896, when it left to join the Scottish Football Combination. This move was seen as a bold choice for the club as the Combination was predominantly a reserve league for those within the SFL and the competition wasn't seen as anything more than that. However, politically it was a good move as it meant that the chairmen in the league would get to know the committees of the clubs within the Combination, so when it came down to election votes, the clubs would more often than not vote for those they were on friendly terms with. While in the Combination, Arthurlie pulled off a great Scottish Cup upset when they beat reigning Scottish league champions Celtic 4-2 in the first round.

In 1901, Arthurlie's risky manoeuvre in joining the Combination paid off when they were elected to the SFL for the first time. Their first match at this level was a great 2-2 draw away to Motherwell, which was followed by a 3-1 home victory over Port Glasgow Athletic. By October, they were doing extremely well in the league, but as winter dawned their form plunged and they slipped down to tenth by the season's end and narrowly avoided the dreaded re-election vote. The following season's form wasn't much better and they ended in ninth position.

Finally, in 1903/04, Arthurlie's luck ran out, and after a dreadful season they ended up in 11th, winning just five times all term. This poor finish meant they faced a re-election vote but, thankfully, they saw off the competition and managed to retain their place within the SFL. After this scare in the summer of 1904, they turned a corner and achieved a respectable sixth place the following season. After a ropey start, they pulled together and ended with more wins than losses for the first time in the SFL. Then the following season they managed to match that record by finishing in sixth again, winning ten matches.

The 1906/07 season was the club's best in its time in league football. They finished in joint second place after a wonderful campaign. However, it started badly and in October they were securely placed in the bottom half of the league. But as 1906 ticked into 1907 things changed and they were performing miracles, ending the season with an eight-match unbeaten run, which took them securely into the top three. They ended up on 27 points, the same as Vale of Leven.

Arthurlie sadly couldn't build on this success, and over the next four years they finished in the bottom three, twice surviving re-election votes with relative ease. They then had some respite in 1911/12 when they climbed to eighth in the league, but this was short-lived, as the following season found them back in a re-election battle, surviving that one too. In 1913/14 they finished in ninth, but by 1914/15 were again back in the bottom two.

The Second Division was abandoned in 1915 due to the ongoing world war. With this, Arthurlie followed most teams from that division in joining the Western League. However, unlike most of the others, when the Second Division returned in 1921, Arthurlie didn't re-join it. After another season in the Western League they applied to return to the Second Division but weren't voted in. However, they wouldn't have to fret for long, as in the summer of 1923 the SFL announced that it would be creating a new Third Division and that the clubs from the Eastern and Western Leagues would be making up most of the numbers.

From the moment it was announced that Arthurlie would enter the Third Division they were seen as one of the main candidates for promotion and they didn't let anyone down. They went on to win 21 matches that season, losing just four times and gaining promotion with ease, five points clear of second place.

Arthurlie were back in the Second Division for the first time in ten years and it saw them safely finish mid-table, in 12th place. The following three seasons saw them finish in seventh place each time but, during the closing months of 1927/28, they were starting to struggle to keep up with the SFL's match guarantees, as their attendances started to drop.

The 1928/29 season was a poor one for the club as they were on the receiving end of some heavy scorelines. It was, though, the off-pitch issues that were beginning to take their toll on the club. As the season started, they had very little cash left over once the match guarantee was paid to their opponents. With this and the overall economic downturn in the country, it was no surprise that they soon started to struggle to make enough money to survive. This was only compounded by the spectator numbers dropping by 66 per cent over the space of five months to an average of around 450 people.

By March 1929, Arthurlie were really struggling, and after a 1-1 draw against St Bernard's at the end of the month, they announced that they were to resign from the SFL as they couldn't meet the required financial needs of the league anymore. This was then confirmed by the league in April 1929 and the club left not only the league but also the SFA.

Once Arthurlie left the league they had a couple of years of inactivity where they played a bit of amateur football, but nothing serious, before they finally agreed to re-form the club as a junior team, holding the same name as the previous senior team. Since that happened in 1931, Arthurlie have gone on to become one of the best junior teams in Scotland. They have won numerous league titles and cups at junior level, including the Scottish Junior Cup on two occasions, and in 2020 they became a senior team again when they joined the West of Scotland League, which will allow them the opportunity of one day making it to the SPFL.

Cambuslang

CAMBUSLANG IS a small commuter town on the edge of Glasgow with a modern-day population of around 30,000. Even though there have been Iron Age remains found within the town, it wasn't until the Industrial Revolution that it began to prosper, mostly as a typical industrial town of the Central Belt area, as mining, farming, steelworks and engine works were all found there. Cambuslang is also famous for being the location where James Beaumont Neilson invented the hot blast in 1828.

Cambuslang Football Club was founded in 1874 as a team called Excelsior (not to be confused with another team called Excelsior from Airdrie), but soon afterwards they were renamed Cambuslang Football Club after, as the story goes, they were challenged by a team from the local village of Halfway to play a football match for the right to call themselves Cambuslang. Excelsior won 4-1 and with it the right to the new name. Now, there isn't any hard evidence to back this claim from the time, just a newspaper column from 1891 saying it happened. Either way, it's a great story.

In 1879, Cambuslang entered the Scottish Cup for the first time, reaching the fifth round, helped in part by being awarded two walkovers, before being put out by Pollokshields Athletic. Prior to 1879, they had taken part in the early stages of the Glasgow Merchants' Charity Cup but barely got past the first round. However, the teams from Lanarkshire saw how popular the cup was, so in 1879 they came together at the Cross Hotel in Hamilton to form the Lanarkshire County Football Association and clubbed together to purchase a cup for their own competition.

Cambuslang went into the early 1880s consistently making it to later rounds of the Scottish Cup but never managing to reach the final. However, during this time they were dominant in the Lanarkshire Cup, winning it in 1884 and 1885 and finishing runners-up four times. But by 1888 the club had fallen out with its fellow Lanarkshire clubs and left to join the much more prosperous Glasgow Football Association.

This first season would be a good one for the club. They played in the first-ever version of the Glasgow Cup and won, beating Rangers 3-1. Then, to add to their already growing reputation, they finally reached the final of the Scottish Cup after defeating Abercorn in a replay by a record score of 10-1 in the semi-final. The final, though, was a lot less glamorous, as in front of 15,000 people they were soundly beaten by Renton, 6-1, a record scoreline for a Scottish Cup Final.

After Cambuslang's success of 1888, the following season was massively anticlimactic, when they were beaten 6-0 in the first round of the Glasgow Cup by Third Lanark. Then, to compound their terrible season, they were beaten 4-1 by

Renton in the Scottish Cup. However, 1889/90 was more respectable when they reached the semi-final of the Glasgow Cup, losing to Celtic, and the fourth round of the Scottish Cup, losing to Dundee East End 3-2 in a replay after the first match, which also ended 3-2 to the team from Dundee, was declared void.

When the meeting was held in March 1890 to form the SFL, Cambuslang were viewed as one of the better teams in the country. This was in no small part due to the fact that they were part of the Glasgow FA rather than the Lanarkshire FA, and not one club from the latter was invited to join the SFL; on the other hand, seven clubs from the Glasgow FA were invited, as well as two from Renfrewshire, three from Dunbartonshire and two from Edinburgh. With Cambuslang having just won the Glasgow Cup and having recently reached the final of the Scottish Cup, it was no surprise that they were invited to the meeting for the formation of the league.

Cambuslang played their first league match on 16 August 1890, beating Vale of Leven 8-2. The next week, they hosted Rangers in front of 4,000 spectators, but were beaten quite convincingly, 6-2. However, the spectators did get to witness the first hat-trick in the SFL, when John McPherson of Rangers scored four times. The rest of Cambuslang's season followed the same pattern as their opening two matches – good wins and bad defeats. When the season ended, they were a very respectable fourth in the league, having won eight matches and lost six, so they were comfortably above the re-election spots.

In 1891/92, Cambuslang had a disastrous season. They got off to a poor start and nothing really changed. In the 22 matches played, they won just two, partly down to losing several of their better players to English teams, including their top scorer. However, this should be caveated, as most clubs in the SFL lost a lot of players after that first season, as English clubs scouted their players, having seen them capable of playing an entire season and offering the better players professional contracts that they snapped up. At the season's end, Cambuslang faced re-election, which turned into a straight-up fight between them and St Mirren, with the Paisley team coming out on top by 12 votes to seven.

After being voted out of the league, Cambuslang applied and were successful in getting into the Scottish Football Alliance, although their luck didn't change, as they again finished rock bottom of the league in that first season. Even in the Scottish Cup, in which they had a proud record, they were poor, being beaten in the first round by Royal Albert 6-1.

For 1893/94, the club even tried to gain membership of the new SFL Second Division but stayed in the Alliance instead, improving their form to finish second behind Royal Albert. At the end of the season they again applied for membership of the Second Division but sadly couldn't find support from anyone. As a result, they stayed in the Alliance until the league was disbanded in 1897.

Cambuslang tried to carry on but money problems were growing by the day. They hadn't been able to play in the Scottish Cup since 1892, and having lost their membership of the SFL and the big gates it attracted, this meant the coffers were almost empty. They still played in the Glasgow Cup and, finally, in 1897, they informed the Glasgow FA of just how bad the financial situation was and were granted £25 to try to ease the pressure. This wasn't enough as they owed more than £100 to a variety of people, a debt that left them with little option but to wind the club up at the end of the year.

During the club's short lifetime, they played at three different grounds. Firstly, Bogshole, between 1874 and 1876, which was nothing more than a pitch laid out on a public park with some rope around the sides to keep the spectators from the playing surface. Their second and slightly more permanent home was Westburn Park, which they occupied between 1876 and 1888. It was here that the club achieved most of its success but they moved in 1888 as they had been ground-sharing with another local team, Cambuslang Hibernian, who continued to use the ground until they were dissolved in 1908. Cambuslang's final home was Whitefield Park, which they used from 1888 until they were wound up in 1897. The pitch was then taken over and is now a bowling club of the same name.

Cambuslang's time playing football was all over within 23 years. However, their legacy has lived on much longer. They still hold three records and the town can be proud of the impact the club had on Scottish football. Today, the only team in Cambuslang is Cambuslang Rangers, but they have no connection to the former team and have spent most of their time in the junior ranks, until 2020 when they joined the West of Scotland League. As for remains of the club, there really isn't anything other than the bowling club at Whitefield Park, which takes up most of the old ground. If you visit the site today you can just about make out a bit of the old terracing to the left-hand side.

Helensburgh

FOR THOSE outside of Scotland, Helensburgh is a picture-postcard Victorian town on the Firth of Clyde, 20 miles outside of Glasgow. It's a lovely small town with big Victorian houses and the sort of place you expect to see steam trains and people in top hats.

The town today isn't a footballing mecca. In fact, apart from an amateur team that plays on a Sunday, it hasn't had a senior or junior footballing team since 1926. However, just because a century has passed doesn't mean that the town was always like that.

In the footballing boom of the Victorian era, Helensburgh had no fewer than five teams playing in the town, those being Helensburgh Victoria, Helensburgh Merchants, Hermitage Former Boys, Helensburgh West-End and Helensburgh FC, on three different occasions.

Now, this is where things get a little bit complicated. The first record of a football team in Helensburgh was in 1874. This team played in that season's Scottish Cup, beating Third Edinburgh RV (who would become St Bernard's in 1878), before losing in the next round to local rivals and eventual runners-up Renton.

The following season they would do even better, getting past another local team, Star of Leven, and then 23rd Renfrew RV, before being put out by Glasgow team, Western. The next season they were knocked out by Vale of Leven in the first round, who would go on to win the cup, then in 1877/78 Helensburgh were again knocked out in the first round.

It would be the Scottish Cup run of 1878/79 that would be the high point in the club's history. In the first round they put four past Kilmarnock Thistle and in the second round they beat local team Alexandria 4-1. In the third round they played Shaugraun, coming out on top 2-0, then in the fourth round they beat Hearts at home 2-1. That win put them into the fifth round for the first time in their history, where they played Hibs away and won 2-1 to secure their place in the next round.

Because of the wonders of the early days of football in Scotland, Helensburgh received a bye into the semi-final of the cup. There they were drawn at home to their local rivals Vale of Leven but weren't destined to make it to Hampden; they were soundly beaten 3-0.

The following season, Helensburgh got through the first round again, before being beaten 7-0 by nearby Dumbarton in the second round. Then, in 1880/81, two teams from Helensburgh entered the Scottish Cup: Helensburgh FC and Helensburgh Victoria. Victoria were soundly beaten by Dumbarton 7-0, while Helensburgh FC got through to the third round before again being beaten by Vale of Leven, this time 4-1.

Both Helensburgh teams again entered the cup in 1881/82, and this was to be the real highlight of football in the town for the next 40 years, as the clubs were drawn to face each other in the second round. However, for reasons that are still unknown, Victoria pulled out of the tie and a walkover was awarded to Helensburgh FC, who went through to face Vale of Leven yet again, and were defeated, yet again.

It was in that season that the first Helensburgh FC folded. The club was struggling to attraact fans, which was in part due to the number of matches a season, often in single figures, meaning they struggled to maintain public interest. The number of clubs in the town and the frequency that they folded was never going to help, and the fact that nearby Dumbarton, Renton and Vale of Leven were the strong local teams with the best local players also took its toll.

Helensburgh also had a much more understandable issue besides the supporter numbers being low. As would become a common theme for a lot of clubs from the smaller towns in those early days, when Helensburgh first entered the Scottish Cup in 1874/75, there were only 25 teams taking part; by the time they played their final match as a club in 1882, that number had increased to 147. These extra teams meant more matches, which was good for income when, at the time, the only other matches available were friendlies. However, it also meant more travelling, which was a slow and expensive experience. As more clubs joined the cup, this meant travelling much greater distances, which had a major impact on a lot of clubs and many pulled out of matches instead of paying to travel, in a time when players weren't professional.

It wasn't long, though, before Helensburgh FC re-formed, in 1885, with the same committee as the previous club, and with the same name and the same kit colours as before. They played one match in 1885 against Dumbarton Athletic in which they were beaten 3-2 at home, before folding again.

Once again, it wasn't too much longer before they were back. After returning in 1886 they mostly played in the junior leagues, amateur football and senior football, but were unable to take part in the Scottish Cup. Most of their matches were sadly only remembered by those chosen few who watched them play on a Saturday afternoon; however, after the First World War, they finally gained full SFA membership.

It was in 1923 that the SFL came up with the idea that would, after 33 years, bring league football to Helensburgh, when it was announced that a third tier would be created. Helensburgh applied and were successful in gaining a place in the league system.

Unfortunately, the league was always destined to fail. To start with, it set a minimum wage for players, which meant that all the clubs were struggling financially before the season even started. Despite this, the league plodded along for three seasons before it was finally dissolved. It was difficult to start with because even though the clubs that got into the league had been successful in the leagues they were in previously, they had only played in their respective local areas. Once the financial burden on teams such as Helensburgh having to travel up to Brechin City, Forfar Athletic or Montrose in Angus one weekend, then a fortnight later having to travel down to the Solway Firth is considered, it becomes clear how much money they would be spending on travelling up and down the country and the subsequent drain on the finances of these small clubs.

Towards the end of the 1925/26 season, it was becoming clearer that the clubs in the league were simply unable to complete the season. This included Helensburgh, who weren't taking the gate money to allow them to survive. On average they would make £20 a week through the turnstiles but to survive they needed a minimum of £30. That was never going to happen and, as a result of the clubs' financial problems, the league was finally called off in mid-April. At this stage Helensburgh were top of the league by one point, having played one match more than nearest challengers Leith Athletic. Unfortunately for Helensburgh, when the league was called off, no champions were declared and the league was fully dissolved, expelling all clubs in the third tier except for Forfar, who were promoted by election to the Second Division.

After the utterly sad affair of league football in the town, Helensburgh folded midway through 1926. This was disappointing as the team was seen as having potential. However, despite people from outside of the town seeming to enjoy the trips to the seaside, the club's committee didn't, and after the failure of league football and them seemingly falling out of love with the game, the club folded, never to return.

Helensburgh played at several grounds but, for the most part, played at Ardencaple Park, which they loaned from the cricket club. They also played at East End Park on East King Street. Ardencaple Park is still there, although it's now a rugby pitch. In the modern day there is an amateur team in the town called Helensburgh Football Club, which was formed in 1981 and plays in the amateur leagues around Glasgow.

When people think about Helensburgh, football really isn't what cones to mind. It's a small town these days of only 15,000 people and you often see several buses taking football fans to Glasgow – I wonder how many of the fans on board will know that their home town once had a team that was playing in the third tier of league football. Also, what's more amazing is that during the six decades between the 1870s and the 1920s, a town of only 8,000 people managed to support no fewer than five teams of their own. It goes to show just how important and infectious football was in those early years.

St Bernard's

THE INTRIGUINGLY named St Bernard's Football Club is the oldest officially formed football club in Edinburgh (Heart of Midlothian Quadrille Assembly Club did play a game of football in December 1873 but this wasn't the Hearts as we know it now, and the Heart of Midlothian Football Club wasn't mentioned in any documentation until July 1874). St Bernard's was formed in February 1874 as Third Edinburgh Rifle Volunteers, and was formed from a group of soldiers from that regiment at the British League of Abstainers Offices a few weeks after watching an exhibition match between Queen's Park and Clydesdale. The team played its first match at the Meadow in Edinburgh, the same place both Hearts and Hibs would start out playing.

The club's early years were spent playing in local and exhibition matches around Edinburgh and Fife. They also have the honour of being the first team from the city to enter the Scottish Cup, in 1874/75, losing 3-0 at Helensburgh in October 1874. The following season they made it to the third round; however, over the next few years they wouldn't make it past round one.

The next major change at the club came in 1878 as they were playing more football, which meant that more of the regiment spent time training or attending football-related activities than turning up at the required military training. That summer, things came to a head when it was reported by the regiment's sergeant major to the commanding officer that the club's latest defeat in the Scottish Cup had a negative impact upon regimental morale, and that since they had been playing in Scottish Cup matches, discipline had begun to slip. The commanding officer took the decision to distance his unit from the football club. After the committee that was running the club was made aware of the military taking a step back, they came together and renamed themselves St Bernard's Football Club after the St Bernard's Well on the Water of Leith.

The changes kept coming, as in 1880 St Bernard's moved to the Royal Gymnasium Ground in the Stockbridge part of the city. Then as the 1880s moved on, the club slipped to becoming the third team in the capital, but despite this kept putting in performances to be proud of, as on three occasions they made it to the fifth round of the Scottish Cup. Meanwhile, as the decade came to an end, Renton wrote to other clubs in Scotland to discuss the creation a Scottish league.

St Bernard's was one of those clubs invited to the meeting in Glasgow that formed the SFL. They voted for the formation of the league; however, they wouldn't take part in the first season, as when it came to the first AGM a few months later, St Bernard's weren't voted into the league by the other clubs. The reason for this was because of professionalism; basically, they were paying players, but unlike Hibs a few years earlier, St Bernard's didn't hide the fact particularly well.

Things came to a head on 16 September 1890 when, after a 7-0 Scottish Cup victory over fellow Edinburgh team Adventurers, their opponents lodged a protest with the SFA over the fact that St Bernard's had recently gained a player, James Ross from Dunfermline Athletic, and that they had obtained him by the fact that they were paying him 10 shillings per match, plus a job in a local biscuit factory. This in itself wasn't suspicious as most clubs at the time before they could legally pay players would offer them well-paid jobs outside of football. However, James Ross was a stonemason and could earn a lot more money from this than he would in a factory.

After a short investigation, the SFA charged St Bernard's with breaching Rule 11 and suspended them until 31 October 1890, removing them from the Scottish Cup. As well as the club Ross was also banned for that period, as well as several committee members. The East of Scotland Football Association came out in support of St Bernard's, claiming double standards in the treatment of the clubs in the west, who were being treated considerably less harshly, and that the SFA only cared about keeping the bigger clubs in the west happy and treating the rest of the country as a mere inconvenience. Why had St Bernard's been banned, whereas teams in the west were at most fined or simply removed from the cup?

St Bernard's were completely unperturbed by the SFA ruling and soon formed a new team called the Edinburgh Saints. This entirely transparent new club went on to play a friendly a week later in which the starting XI contained nine players from St Bernard's. Most of the clubs in Scotland felt sorry for St Bernard's, even in Glasgow, which meant that there was a near never-ending list of teams willing to play Edinburgh Saints in friendlies. One of these was Renton, and on 27 September Edinburgh Saints travelled there, despite Renton playing against the advice of the SFA and the SFL.

Within three days of that friendly, both clubs were hauled up in front of the SFA, accused of professionalism, and in a completely draconian measure both Renton and St Bernard's (the SFA had refused Edinburgh Saints membership as it was obvious the club was merely St Bernard's trying to get around the SFA's previous warning) were expelled, as were the Edinburgh Saints' committee members and the players who took part in the tie until 30 April 1891.

This SFA ruling put the East of Scotland Football Association in an awkward position as they had permitted the Edinburgh Saints to form and allowed them to play, mostly in support of what they viewed as St Bernard's being harshly punished by the SFA originally. However, as the SFA had treated Edinburgh Saints and St Bernard's as one and the same, the East of Scotland FA felt they had no choice but to regrettably remove the membership of Edinburgh Saints and refund them their membership money. So, on 8 October, Edinburgh Saints were wound up. This was a club that had existed for a little over two weeks but had caused more controversy than most teams would manage in 50 years.

This saga had another twist to go before it came to an end. In mid-November, some six weeks after the Renton and

Edinburgh Saints were suspended, nine clubs (Dumbarton, Hibernian, Celtic, Clyde, Third Lanark, Abercorn, Hearts, St Mirren and Cowlairs) lodged a protest on their behalf about the treatment they had received from the SFA. The SFA wouldn't back down, though, and dismissed the protest. After that, St Bernard's took the decision to simply sit out their ban and reapplied to the SFA on 1 May 1891, when they regained their membership and put an end to the sorry saga. While they sat tight for those seven months, Renton took the SFA to the Court of Session in Edinburgh and won their case.

St Bernard's welcomed their fans back as a completely legit member of the SFA by playing a friendly on 21 May 1891 against Renton, losing 2-1. In the summer, St Bernard's became founding members of the Scottish Football Alliance, while Renton, thanks to their court case, were readmitted to the SFL after having spent a couple of seasons finishing fourth and second in the Scottish Football Alliance. Meanwhile, St Bernard's applied in the summer, at the AGM of the SFL, for league membership but failed at their first attempt. However, the following summer they were successful and entered the SFL for the 1893/94 season.

They lined up for the first time as a league team on 19 August 1893 against Third Lanark, losing 5-3 after leading 3-0 at one point. However, they went on to have a great season, taking points from Celtic, Rangers and Dumbarton, all recent champions of Scotland. Their successes in the league were, however, dampened by their exit from the Scottish Cup, beaten 8-1 by Celtic in the third round. A few weeks later, though, St Bernard's regained some honour by beating St

Mirren 8-3 in the league. Their good performances in the league saw them finish in third place, three points ahead of Rangers.

In 1894/95, St Bernard's had their moment in the sun. The league started with defeats to Celtic and Rangers, before going on good runs and ending the season in a comfortable sixth place. This season, though, their form came in the Scottish Cup. They beat Airdrieonians 4-2 in the first round before hosting Kilmarnock in the second round, beating them 3-1. In the quarter-final they defeated Clyde 6-2; however, the match was declared a friendly as the pitch was in terrible condition. However, that made little difference as in the replay St Bernard's won 2-1. In the semi-final they met fellow Edinburgh team Hearts. The match ended 0-0 and was dragged into a replay where in the second half St Bernard's scored the only goal to put them through to their first-ever Scottish Cup Final.

On 20 April 1895 St Bernard's lined up at Ibrox Park in Glasgow in front of some 12,000 spectators to take on none other than old friends Renton in the Scottish Cup Final. St Bernard's were by now overwhelming favourites for the cup as it was some surprise that Renton had made it through to the final. On a stunning day, St Bernard's took control of the match with two quick-fire goals in the first half before, against the run of play, Renton grabbed one back just on the stroke of half-time. In the second half, the pressure St Bernard's expected from Renton never really came until the final five minutes, but even when it did their backline held firm and they won the cup more easily than the scoreline would have people believe.

The year 1895 would be one of the best for football in Edinburgh. When St Bernard's returned to the city with the cup they were met by thousands in the streets and treated to a banquet. This year saw all major trophies in Scotland being held in the city of Edinburgh, as Hearts won the First Division title, St Bernard's won the Scottish Cup and Hibernian won the Second Division title for the second time in a row, gaining promotion through the election vote.

The following season, St Bernard's strongly defended the Scottish Cup, making it to the final four before being beaten by Hearts, 1-0. Hearts would go on to play Hibernian in the final played at New Logie Green in Edinburgh, which was at the time the home ground of St Bernard's. Hearts won 3-1 in the only Scottish Cup Final played outside of Glasgow.

While their cup performances were very good, in the league things were starting to slip for St Bernard's. During the rest of the decade they ended each season in the bottom half of the league, including facing a re-election vote in 1897/98 after finishing in ninth place. The following season they climbed to seventh, but this improvement was short-lived, as they then finished ninth again and faced another re-election vote. This time they lost the vote, so after seven seasons in the First Division St Bernard's were relegated to the Second Division.

Once a club slipped into the Second Division it was normal for those voted down to continue to fall away for a few seasons before sorting themselves out and moving back up. This was in part because of a losing mentality and more commonly because the best players were picked off and often abandoned the club. However, St Bernard's went against the grain and spent money to try to bounce straight back up to the top flight. They had a great season and ended as Second Division champions, having lost only three matches. However, things weren't so easy, as at the summer's AGM they weren't voted into the top flight, despite their great form, which was as much a shock to them as the fact that neither Hearts nor Hibs voted for their fellow Edinburgh club.

In the aftermath of this failed attempt at returning to the top flight, St Bernard's lost most of their best players and they slowly slipped down the league standings, finishing sixth, then fifth, before in the 1903/04 season committee member and money man William Lapsley was killed in a road accident. With the loss of their backer, they then finished in eighth place, before in 1904/05 ending the season with their worst finish – bottom of the league, winning just three times all season. However, at the re-election vote they were saved with relative ease and lived to fight another day in the league.

With the scare of the uncertainty of the re-election vote in 1904/05, St Bernard's reorganised for the following season and put in a fantastic performance, finishing in a very respectable fifth place. In 1906/07, there was an even greater improvement and they won the Second Division for the second time in six years. Therefore, that summer's election vote was an attempt to get back to the top flight and not for survival. Again, though, they couldn't gain enough support and were condemned to the second tier.

The disappointment of the failed vote stung the club hard, and over the next couple of seasons they dropped to eighth in the league. In 1909/10 they revived and climbed to third, but after that they finished mid-table for the next four seasons, without ever challenging at the top or being near the bottom.

As the First World War loomed large in the 1914/15 season, St Bernard's climbed brilliantly, winning 18 matches and finishing the season in a solid third place in the league. However, the war took priority and the Second Division was suspended. St Bernard's therefore moved into the Eastern League and finished second behind Armadale. After two seasons they, like many others, stopped playing for the duration of the war.

During the hostilities many footballers entered the armed forces and those at St Bernard's were no different. Fifteen players from the club saw some form of active service and several never returned, including John Ferguson, who was killed by a grenade at the Battle of Le Transloy in October 1916 during the final major attack of the Battle of the Somme. He was mentioned in dispatches and recommended for the Victoria Cross. He was just 24 years old.

When the war ended and the Second Division wasn't restarted in 1919, St Bernard's joined the Central League instead. They stayed there for two seasons, finishing in mid-table on both occasions. Finally, in 1921, the SFL brought back the second tier and made the league up from the teams from the Central League, which brought St Bernard's back into the Second Division once more.

However, their return to league football wasn't overly spectacular. They finished 1921/22 in ninth place, before slipping into the bottom three for the next couple of seasons, narrowly avoiding relegation to the Third Division. As the

1920s progressed, they gradually improved year on year, climbing up the division. Finally, in 1928/29, they made it up to sixth place. However, the next two seasons saw them drop back into mid-table mediocrity.

In the 1930s, St Bernard's started to find form again. After a high finish in 1931/32 of fifth, they dropped again to mid-table, but by 1934/35 they were on the rise, finishing in third, missing out on promotion by just three points, having scored 103 goals during the process. The following season they again dropped to fifth place but still scored 106 goals. However, in 1936/37 they finished just outside the promotion places, in third, missing out by just three points again, having scored 100 goals during the season.

As the decade continued, war clouds were beginning to gather over Europe, while in Edinburgh, St Bernard's kept putting in great performances in the league and reached a Scottish Cup semi-final. By the end of 1938/39 they had fallen to seventh in a very tight league but as 1939/40 kicked off they seemed to be in a good position to fight for promotion. Unfortunately, the political situation overtook football and, after just four matches of the season, the league was suspended. St Bernard's moved to the Eastern League, which was also suspended in 1940, so they moved to the North Eastern League for two seasons, playing their final match of that season on 16 May 1942.

A few months after that match, one of the club's committee members, a director, died, and it was announced that the executor of the will wanted one of the loans given to the club repaid immediately. With no league matches, no cash reserves and no players to be sold, the club was left with just one choice, which was to sell their home ground, the Royal Gymnasium Ground, which had been their home since 1900.

Soon after this, St Bernard's became homeless, so they made an approach to merge with Leith Athletic; however, this approach was rejected, although Leith did purchase a stand from St Bernard's. In 1946, St Bernard's, without a home or players, entered the Scottish Qualifying Cup but never played the match. Shortly afterwards, the remaining members of the committee came together to formally wind the club up. After 68 years of history they finally gave up the ghost, being homeless, penniless and without a player to their name. St Bernard's Football Club, a team that had won the Second Division twice and won a Scottish Cup in 1895, finally closed, leaving its mark on history.

The club's name would continue as the St Bernard's Supporters' Club formed a boys' club in 1947, which is still going to this day. However, the St Bernard's Supporters' Club folded in 1951, giving the money it had collected over the years to the boys' club and to the St Bernard's Cup, which is a competition for primary schools in Edinburgh. As well as the boys' club and the cup competition, there have been several amateur teams over the years that have taken on the St Bernard's name, but none have taken it back into the senior leagues yet.

King's Park

THE STORY of King's Park Football Club is one of a club that fell victim to circumstance more than being wronged by an owner, when on the night of 19/20 July 1940 one of only two bombs to be dropped on the city of Stirling in the entire war landed on the north terracing of the Forthbank Stadium.

The football club formed in 1875 and, as with a lot of Scottish clubs from around this time, there is almost no way of confirming the exact date of formation, but 1875 is the generally accepted date. They get their name from the King's Park area of Stirling, where the club's committee first met. Even though they were formed in this area, they didn't stay there long, and by 1879 they were playing at Forthbank Park, later to become the Forthbank Stadium. They would remain there for the rest of their existence.

King's Park, like most other clubs around that time, started life playing in friendlies, including ties against Queen's Park, Third Lanark, Dumbarton, Vale of Leven, Blackburn Olympic and Darwin, amongst others. It wasn't until the 1879/80 season that they first took part in the Scottish Cup.

In 1890, as the SFL was established and 12 of the country's most prominent clubs were invited to attend that meeting in Glasgow to establish a league, King's Park were furious at not being invited. So, in 1891, they, along with Airdrieonians, Ayr, East Stirlingshire, Morton, Kilmarnock, Linthouse, Northern, Partick Thistle, Port Glasgow Athletic, St Bernard's and Thistle, met to form the Scottish Football Alliance.

The Alliance, in different forms, existed on and off right up until 1957, when it was finally disbanded. However, it was condemned to never really put up a successful fight against the SFL, as the country's biggest clubs from the biggest cities were in the latter, plus, in the early days of organised leagues, players could move incredibly easily, and the SFL allowed professionalism legally from 1893. All the clubs had two sets of books prior to that date, one for inspection from the league to show all players were amateur, and one that was the actual books which showed players' wages.

The Scottish Football Alliance was also handicapped when, in 1892, due to teams not having set fixture lists and often opting to play in more glamorous and lucrative friendlies instead of playing league matches, a large number of the founding members left and began negotiations with the SFL to create a second tier of Scottish football. This second tier came into existence in 1893 and between then and 1897, when the Alliance was first disbanded (only to come back in 1905 but as a sort of reserve league for the bigger teams), almost all Alliance teams joined the SFL.

King's Park didn't. They did leave the Scottish Football Alliance in 1892 but no reason is given. It's argued that it may have been financial as they were the furthest north team and the price of travelling to matches was prohibitive for a club that was struggling to pull in the fans. Another reason could be that in 1891, in a meeting in Larbert just to the south of Stirling, several clubs from Clackmannanshire and Fife met to create the Midland Football League. The clubs that night were Alloa Athletic, Alva, Bridge of Allan, Camelon, Clackmannan, Cowdenbeath, Dunblane, Dunfermline Athletic, Grangemouth and Raith Rovers. In 1892, both King's Park and East Stirlingshire joined the league.

In 1892/93, King's Park won the Midland Football League, their only league title in their entire existence. While playing in this league, they also had their best run in the Scottish Cup, beating Lochee United 5-2 in the first round and then Dumbarton 2-1 at home, before going out in the quarter-final to Hearts 4-2.

In 1897, the Midland Football League merged with the Central Football League (a league of teams from the same area) to form the Central Football Combination. King's Park stayed with the league until 1905/06, when for one season they re-joined the Scottish Football Alliance, but soon after they joined the Scottish Football Union until 1909, when they, along with most of the founding members of the Midland Football League, helped to re-form the Central Football League, remaining there until the outbreak of the First World War.

After the war the SFL stated that they wouldn't be bringing back the second tier. So, in 1919, the Central Football League returned, and so did Kings Park, but only for a short period, in 1921/22, the SFL brought back the second tier and this time King's Park were allowed to join, and in doing so would remain there until 1939.

King's Park became a solid mid-table Second Division team. They made the headlines on 20 October 1923 when they played Dundee Hibernian in a 3-2 loss at home, because two days later Dundee Hibernian would change their name to Dundee United.

King's Park's best season in the league was in 1927/28 when they lost out on promotion by just one point to Third Lanark, finishing third in the league, scoring an impressive 84 goals in the season. A couple of years later they started setting records. First was a 12-2 league victory over Forfar Athletic on 2 January 1930, when Jim Dyet scored eight goals on his debut for the club, a British record to this day. Then, in January and February of 1932, Alex Haddow scored five league hat-tricks in consecutive matches.

For the rest of the 1930s, King's Park remained distinctly mid-table in the second tier of Scottish football. During this period, Hugh MacPherson, father of legendary football commentator Archie, played for the club, as did the father of former Scotland manager Craig Brown.

When the Second World War broke out in the autumn of 1939 all professional football leagues were suspended. King's Park did play a few wartime friendlies, which included guest players such as Andy Black and Bob and Bill Shankly, amongst other famous names. Then, in 1940, they were approached to join a new Midland Football League, but when Dundee pulled out the attraction was gone, and the league didn't start. As a result, the managing director of King's Park, Tom Ferguson, put the club into a temporary hiatus.

This break was made somewhat more permanent when, on the night of 19/20 July 1940, that Luftwaffe pilot dropped his bomb. He was returning from a raid on the docks of Clydeside when he released the bombs over the outskirts of Stirling to lighten the return flight. The first bomb fell harmlessly on to a field, just upturning some potatoes; the other fell on to the northern terracing of the Forthbank Stadium, destroying it and leaving a 30-foot crater in the pitch. The pitch was sufficiently repaired to play a few 'loose' matches, but it was obvious that it would never do. In 1944, King's Park had its application their join the North Eastern League turned down due to a lack of stadium facilities.

After the bombing and with allegations of how the wartime players were paid by the club, it was decided to fold King's Park. Football wouldn't be missing for long, though, as in 1945 Stirling Albion was formed, with former King's Park director Tom Ferguson taking a major role in the forming of the new club.

Even though the club had folded during the war they weren't wound up until 1953, when the war office finally settled the claim from them over the bomb damage inflicted in 1940. The payment was made to Stirling Albion. As for the stadium, Stirling Albion FC purchased an estate and built Annfield Stadium, where the club would remain until 1992, when they moved to the Forthbank Stadium where they play to this day, around half a mile away from the original Forthbank Stadium.

In the modern day, Stirling Albion play in the SPFL at this same stadium, an amazing wee ground, with stunning views of the Wallace Monument in the distance and highly worth a visit.

Cowlairs

THERE ARE in Scotland very few teams that were formed from railway companies. In England there are a countless number, including, most famously, Manchester United. In Scotland it's different, with Cowlairs being one of the few exceptions to that rule.

Cowlairs Football Club was formed in 1876 by workers from Hyde Park and Cowlairs Railway Works in Springburn, which is still to this day a predominantly working-class area of Glasgow, just to the north of the centre.

During the 1870s the local employment was mainly the railway works. These would finally close down in 2019, ending 163 years of engine works in the Springburn area of the city.

Cowlairs had a fairly quiet start to life. For the most part, in their early years they spent their time playing other local teams and were viewed by many in the establishment of Scottish football as more junior-level rather than a senior team. This is despite the club never actually claiming an interest in being either a junior- or senior-level team.

In 1880 Cowlairs made their first appearance in the Scottish Cup. After having some success in the early rounds, they went out in a tight match to St Mirren, 1-0. The following season they entered the cup again, drawing Queen's Park. In the first match Cowlairs gained a very credible 2-2 draw, and were in fact unlucky not to win as they were leading going into the dying seconds of the match. In the replay they were defeated 9-0 by a Queen's team that clearly had learned from their previous mistakes.

Over the next few years Cowlairs went out of the cup in the early rounds on each occasion. While they never got overly far in the competition, they did rack up some impressive scorelines during that time, including a 13-0 win over Apsley, an 18-2 victory over Temperance Athletic and a spectacular 21-1 success over Helensburgh Victoria.

To the surprise of many, Cowlairs was one of the clubs invited to the meeting to help form the SFL in March 1890. This was fairly remarkable for a club that was neither one of the founding members of the SFA nor had got further than the fifth round of the cup during their time. However, invited they were, and they made their bow in the SFL on 16 August 1890, when they got a credible 1-1 draw away to Dumbarton. The following weekend they had their first-ever home match (played at Celtic Park because of stadium requirements), where they beat Vale of Leven 3-2 in a brilliant end-to-end encounter.

Despite the early promise that August seemed to provide, the honeymoon period for the club was already over. In September, both they and Celtic were deducted four points for playing ineligible players. Then in October Cowlairs were placed under investigation for financial mismanagement. Finally, in November they were temporarily suspended by both the SFA and the league due to their maladministered books. The ban was lifted in mid-December but, due to no pitch maintenance, the ground was unplayable for league matches until the turn of the year.

By the end of that first season, Cowlairs had picked up a mere six points from 18 matches, finishing the season bottom of the league; even without the points deduction they would still have been bottom. This meant they faced the uncertainty of having to be re-elected back into the league. As the re-election loomed large the SFA released its findings into the financial conduct of many clubs. Most came through it fine; a few were given warnings. However, Cowlairs were given special condemnation for 'specially written up books'. With this ringing in the other clubs' ears, it was no surprise to see that Cowlairs weren't re-elected. Instead, Clyde and Leith Athletic were voted in, as well as Renton regaining their place in the league.

As 1891/92 started, Cowlairs found themselves without a league to play in. This, while not being good for the gate numbers, did have the added benefit of allowing them to be successful in the Scottish Cup, where they got through to the quarter-finals before being defeated by eventual champions Celtic 4-1. The 1892/93 season saw Cowlairs again try to get back into the SFL, but they picked up zero votes, so instead joined the rival league, the Scottish Football Alliance. They won that division by a clear seven points over nearest rivals St Bernard's, and it came as no surprise that at the end of the season they tried to get in the SFL but again they failed.

This failure was short-lived as less than a month later the SFL announced that they would be starting a Second Division. For 1893/94 the Second Division was mostly made up of the clubs from the Scottish Football Alliance, Cowlairs included. That season was the best league season Cowlairs would have, finishing second, two points behind champions Hibs. During the season they won 13 matches, scoring 72 times. However, the cup wasn't so good for the club, as they were beaten 8-0 by Rangers. At the end of the season neither Cowlairs nor Hibs were voted into the top flight; instead it was third-placed Clyde who got the votes to be promoted.

After the success of their first season in the second tier there were some understandably high hopes for Cowlairs going into the second season. Sadly, this didn't come about as they finished rock bottom, winning a mere two matches of 18 and ending with just seven points. When it came to the re-election vote they were voted out in favour of Kilmarnock and Linthouse.

In 1895/96, Cowlairs played only a few friendlies. By now it was common knowledge how badly run the club was, both financially and administratively, and very few leagues would allow them access. By the end of that season, their debts were mounting, most of the players had moved away and even in friendlies they were struggling to field a team. Inevitably, by August 1896, the debts were so high that, even after some futile last-ditch attempts to find a league, the club was finally dissolved.

During their 20 years Cowlairs had become founder members of the league and produced a few Scotland internationals, including John McPherson, who would go on to play for Everton, Kilmarnock, and then Rangers for 12 years.

During its existence, the club spent its time between Gourlay Park and Springvale Park, both sadly no longer with us. Springvale Park was soon taken over and turned into a massive railway siding, which it still is today. Gourlay Park was built over too, and unfortunately nothing remains of this ground either. In the modern era nothing is left of Cowlairs within the Springburn area, where the footballing torch was taken over by Petershill, a junior team, in 1897. Petershill have no direct link to Cowlairs or the other local club from that time, Northern, but Petershill are still going strong to this day.

Abercorn

THESE DAYS when we think of Paisley and football, most people, rightly, think of only St Mirren, the club that has represented the town of Paisley for more than 140 years. In 1877, the year that St Mirren was founded, another club from the town was established just a few months later.

Abercorn Football Club was founded in November of that year in the east end of the town, with a membership of around 200 people. They played their first match, a 1-1 draw in December, against the 79th Highland Reserve Volunteers. By June 1878, Abercorn and 17 other clubs from Renfrewshire met at the Star Hotel in Paisley to form the Renfrewshire County Football Association and clubbed together to purchase a cup for the competition.

It wasn't until 1880 that Abercorn made their first appearance in the Scottish Cup, when on 18 September they defeated local team Barrhead 7-1 in the first round, then beat Morton in the second round 4-1, before being put out by rivals St Mirren 4-1 in round three.

By 1887/88 Abercorn had a reputation of being involved in high-scoring matches. Prior to this they had reached the fifth round of the Scottish Cup twice after usually coming unstuck in the third round. However, in 1887/88 they got through to the semi-final, en route to which they registered two 9-0 wins. It would be the semi-final, though, that would make history. Abercorn were drawn against Cambuslang, the match played in Paisley ending 1-1, thus forcing a replay in Cambuslang a week later. There, on 21 January 1888, the two teams faced off again, the match ending Cambuslang 10 Abercorn 1, which is still a record scoreline for a Scottish Cup semi-final.

During the period from 1886 to the formation of the SFL, Abercorn were the dominant Renfrewshire team. They reached at least the fourth round of the Scottish Cup each season and won the Renfrewshire Cup in 1886, 1887, 1889 and 1890. By March 1890, when the invitations were sent out for the clubs to form a league, it was no surprise to anyone for Abercorn to be invited, as they had in that season again been in the final four of the Scottish Cup, this time going out to Queen's Park in much more respectable fashion, 2-0.

Abercorn played their first SFL match on 30 August 1890, a fortnight after the rest of the league had kicked off. They travelled to Vale of Leven, where they were defeated 2-1. Two weeks later they played their first-ever home league match, against Renton, winning 4-2. A week later they played their first Paisley derby against St Mirren, losing 4-2 away. That first season of league football was a mix for Abercorn. They finished seventh in the league, one place and one point above rivals St Mirren, but more importantly one place above the spots needing to seek a re-election vote. Their season ended with five wins, two draws and 11 losses. While this league form wasn't the greatest, the cups were just as much of a mixed bag. In the Renfrewshire Cup, Abercorn went out in the second round to St Mirren. However, in the Scottish Cup, for the second season running they reached the semi-finals, before being beaten by league champions Dumbarton 3-1.

The 1891/92 season got off to an indifferent start for Abercorn with an 8-1 defeat at the hands of Dumbarton, before things improved to bring some balance. They again finished one place above St Mirren and one place above the re-election spots, and in the cups, results were again mixed. In the Scottish Cup Abercorn went out in the first round to Queen's Park, whereas in the Renfrewshire Cup they got through to the final at Cappielow, where they faced St Mirren. After being one down for a large portion of the match, in the dying moments, Abercorn turned the score around and won their fifth and final Renfrewshire Cup.

In 1892/93 Abercorn's luck in the league finally started to run out. They didn't pick up a point in their first eight matches and, despite a spirited fightback at the end of the season, they finished second bottom, some six points from the safety, so facing a re-election vote. At that season's league AGM, Abercorn finished fifth in the vote and, as a result, were voted out of the league. Luckily, though, their time out of the league was short-lived, as in July the SFL announced that enough interest had been shown to allow a Second Division to be created.

Abercorn were thus founding members of the Second Division. However, a season that offered so much hope and success was a disappointment from start to finish. They lost four of their five first outings and their luck wasn't much better in the cups, going out in the early rounds in both the Scottish Cup and Renfrewshire Cup. At the season's end Abercorn finished just one place from re-election. The following season was even worse as they finished in the re-election spot, although they successfully maintained their place in the Second Division.

Thankfully, 1895/96 saw a massive turnaround for Abercorn. Completely unexpectedly, they topped the league early in the season and stayed there, champions by four points, winning 13 matches en route and scoring 55 goals. At the end of the season the top three teams in the second tier went up against the bottom three in the top tier in an election and Abercorn were voted into the top flight, as Dumbarton went the other way.

However, Abercorn's time back in the top tier was extremely short-lived, and to say 1896/97 was a let-down would be an understatement. They won just one match and gained one draw all season, to end on a miserable three points. At the end of the season they faced another re-election vote and, completely unsurprisingly, after such a shocking season, didn't get re-elected. After just one season Abercorn were back in the second tier.

The club's return to the Second Division didn't see an upturn in results; rather, in that first season back, 1897/98, they finished in seventh place. The following season was even worse for the Paisley club, as they finished bottom of the league and had to go through the uncertainty of re-election again. This time, though, they were comfortably voted back into the league. After this scare of re-election, however, Abercorn began to climb up the league again, finishing

1899/1900 in sixth, only to better this the following season by finishing third.

This would turn out to be the high point for the club, as in the next six seasons they finished in the bottom three and faced re-election. In 1906/07, they managed to climb up to ninth, their highest finish since 1900/01. Then 1907/08 saw a huge improvement when they finished in a very respectable fourth. However, in 1908/09, they had a poor start to the season, winning none of their opening three matches, but they soon improved. They went on to win 13 of their next 19 matches and were crowned Second Division champions, winning the title by three points over nearest challengers Raith Rovers. Despite being champions, they decided against applying for election to the First Division, opting to remain in the second tier.

Abercorn had a positive start to 1909/10 and topped the league at the start of November. However, they couldn't maintain this and ended up ten points adrift of the leaders, down in fifth place. Then followed another poor season in 1910/11 when they finished joint eighth with Arthurlie, Dundee Hibernian and Port Glasgow Athletic. The following campaign saw a turnaround for Abercorn, as they finished second behind Ayr United and ended the season with the division's best defensive record. The next few seasons saw Abercorn gain a couple of very respectable fourth- and fifth-place finishes in the league.

Thus, at the outbreak of the First World War in August 1914, Abercorn were a comfortable mid-table team, but the 1914/15 season would be their last in the SFL. When the season came to an end in the summer of 1915, attendances throughout Scotland were drastically low. The horrors of the front and of the deaths of the children and loved ones of local people made footballers the targets of everyone. Why was it acceptable that people's children could be slaughtered at the front, when these perfectly healthy, fit young men were just running around a field for fun? What's the difference?

Abercorn ended that season in 12th place but they didn't need to worry about re-election as the SFL disbanded the Second Division due to the conflict. They therefore entered the Western League along with many other clubs from the Second Division, where they stayed until 1920. During this period in the Western League, Abercorn's best finish was fourth in 1916.

By the end of the 1919/20 season Abercorn were in the bottom two of the Western League. This, though, was the least of their problems. Ever since their formation in 1877 they had led a somewhat nomadic life and at no point in their history spent more than ten years at any one ground. Their first home was East Park until 1879, when they moved to Blackstoun Park. Then after ten years they moved again, this time to Underwood Park. In 1899 they moved to Old Ralston Park on East Lane, where they remained until 1909, when they relocated a short distance to New Ralston Park. In 1919 the landlords decided to not renew Abercorn's lease on the ground, leaving them homeless. The club and its supporters believed that the St Mirren committee had some part to play in this with its connections to the local council but nothing has ever been proved to justify this argument.

Abercorn existed as a club for a further few seasons, although they never played another match. Finally, their membership of the SFA ended when the Association disbarred them in 1922 due to the lack of a stadium. The reality was that the club was effectively defunct from 1920 when it lost its stadium, so this came as no surprise. However, they continued to have an annual dinner in Paisley right up until 1939, but no phoenix club was ever considered.

In modern times there is very little to remind people that Abercorn played in Paisley; there is a street named after the club but that's about it. The stadium was turned first into an ice rink and is now a supermarket. Even the train station called Abercorn closed in 1967.

Today, Paisley is a proud one-club town, with St Mirren having won the Scottish Cup and League Cup in the not-too-distant past. It's a surprise, though, that in a town with such a high population, another team hasn't emerged since the demise of Abercorn over 100 years ago. Even though they had a torrid time of it with a lack of stadium facilities and their incredible inconsistency over their time in the leagues, they should be remembered better than they currently are for their vital role in the creation of the SFL.

Airdrieonians

AIRDRIE IS a well-known industrial town in the Central Belt of Scotland. The town found within the Monklands district is famous for being hard-working and is intrinsically linked to heavy industry and mining. However, it has been hit hard by the economic downturn in the years since heavy industry fell away.

The town's football team was Airdrieonians Football Club, formed as Excelsior Football Club in 1878 but changing its name in 1881. This was the original club, which folded in 2002. The current Airdrieonians was originally founded as Airdrie United and was called that until 2013 when they received permission to take over the Airdrieonians name.

The original club first entered the Scottish Cup in 1879/80 as Excelsior and made it through to the third round, before going out 7-1 at the hands of Hamilton Academical. However, this would be the high point for some time, as they then struggled to get past the second round for most of the 1880s, during which they suffered some terrible defeats, including a 10-2 humbling against Cambuslang. The one exception to this was in 1885/86, when the club, now Airdrieonians, made it to the fourth round, losing to Queen's Park 1-0. En route, they registered a fantastic 15-2 victory over Cambuslang Hibernian in the second round and an 8-2 win against Tollcross in the third.

For the rest of the decade, Airdrieonians failed to get past the fourth round, but did start to have more respectable performances and show as the predominant team in the Airdrie area. By the time the 1890s started, they and Albion Rovers were the main two teams in the Monklands district.

After the SFL was formed in 1890, Airdrieonians, along with several other clubs, formed the Scottish Football Alliance the following year. They remained in the Alliance until the summer of 1894, when they were elected to the SFL Second Division. Over the next eight seasons, they stayed safely in mid-table, rarely challenging at the top but, equally, not facing the uncertainty of a re-election vote in the bottom half of the league either.

The 1902/03 season was a brilliant one for Airdrieonians. They started with a run of nine straight wins to put them top of the league and they never let this form drop. They lost just two matches all season and won the league title by seven points. At the end of the season they felt comfortable about their chances of being promoted at that summer's AGM and it turned out to be fairly easy, as they and second-placed Motherwell both eased through the AGM by gaining the highest number of votes.

With 1903/04 being Airdrieonians' first season in the top flight of Scottish football, after an indifferent start they steadied to end up in a respectable 11th place in the standings. If that first season in the top tier was respectable, the second was fantastic, as they finished in fourth place. While they were some seven points behind Third Lanark in third, it was still a good return for a club that had only been in the top league for two seasons.

Over the next few campaigns, Airdrieonians continued their good league finishes, coming third and fourth, before dropping down in 1907/08 to sixth. Then, as the 1900s wore on, they slowly slipped down, finishing consistently in mid-table. However, just prior to the First World War, they started to regain form and achieved a couple of high-end finishes.

When the war broke out in 1914 the SFL continued but by the summer of 1915 the Second Division had been suspended. For Airdrieonians, the war leagues were mixed to say the least, as between 1914/15 and 1919/20 they achieved finishes of 11th, 15th, 4th, 15th, 13th and 7th.

Post-war, and as the 1920s dawned, Airdrieonians were about to hit their prime. The decade started with a disappointing 16th-place finish in 1921/22 and the following season started similarly, with disappointing results. Soon, though, things began to improve when in September they purchased 18-year-old Hughie Gallacher from Queen of the South. With the creativity of the small, feisty attacker, they went on to finish in second place in the league, five points behind champions Rangers.

Then 1923/24 was the club's best-ever season. To start with, they boosted their attacking forces with the signing of Bob McPhail, who quickly set up a formidable striking partnership with the already-settled Gallacher. This duo helped fire Airdrieonians up to second in the league again and propelled them through on a wonderful Scottish Cup run.

After easing through the early rounds, Airdrieonians were taken to a second replay by Ayr United in the quarter-final, before finally going through with a 1-0 win. In the semi-final they beat Falkirk 3-1 to reach the final. On 19 April 1924, Airdrieonians lined up in their first-ever Scottish Cup Final, against a Hibernian team that had been there many times before. In the match played at Ibrox in front of over 60,000 people, Willie Russell scored twice in the first half to put Airdrieonians in a comfortable position, and Hibs never really fought back, allowing the Diamonds to win their only-ever Scottish Cup with relative ease.

For 1924/25, Airdrieonians managed to keep a hold of their potent attacking force of Gallacher, McPhail and Russell. This allowed the team to score 85 times in the league, making them the highest-scoring team in the division. As the season came to a close, they had pushed Rangers all the way and finished in second place for the third season running, missing out on the title by just three points. In the Scottish Cup they defended their title well until a third-round defeat, 3-1 by Dundee, who would go on to reach the cup final before losing to Celtic.

In the summer of 1925, Airdrieonians went on a tour of Norway and Sweden, which was a huge success and led to the forming of supporters' clubs in both countries. Up until the Second World War local papers in those countries carried Airdrieonians' results.

As the 1925/26 season started, the club's brilliant attacking line started to get picked off. First to go was Willie Russell, who in September left to join Preston North End; then in December came a massive loss, as Newcastle United paid

£6,500 for the services of Hughie Gallacher. With the loss of two members of its famous front three it was no surprise that Airdrieonians' good early-season form didn't hold, although they still finished second, albeit some eight points behind Celtic and ahead of Hearts only by goal difference.

After finishing second four seasons in a row, Airdrieonians then slipped to fourth place in 1926/27, and then, to compound things, in the summer of 1927 they lost Bob McPhail to Rangers for £5,000. With the loss of the last member of their potent front line, they gradually fell into mid-table and stopped challenging at the top end of the league.

When the 1930s started, Airdrieonians were falling away even further and on two occasions only narrowly avoided relegation, finishing one place above the drop. Finally, though, in 1935/36 they were relegated. Having lost 20 matches that season, they fell out of the First Division for the first time in over 30 years, by just one point.

When they dropped into the Second Division they put up a good fight to return to the top flight, but as was common for many clubs, external issues were taking over the game on the pitch. In the three seasons prior to the Second World War, Airdrieonians finished in fourth, third and fourth respectively, missing out on promotion in each season by single-digit points totals. Finally, after just four matches of the new season, the league was suspended because of the conflict.

During the war years, Airdrieonians entered the Western League but mostly spent their time playing in friendlies or the Wartime Cup. Post-war they entered the B Division, which was the renamed the Second Division. In 1946/47, eight years after the last league season, they finished second behind Dundee but still some 11 points clear of third-placed East Fife.

However, after just one season back in the top flight, they were relegated, which was the start of a decade where they were promoted and relegated seven times. However, after they won the B Division title in 1954/55, they went on to spend the next ten years in the top flight, but never finishing above ninth in the process.

Airdrieonians were relegated in 1964/65 but bounced straight back up the following season and remained stable in the bottom half of the league until the turn of the 1970s. In 1972/73, they were relegated again, but once more returned at the first attempt, winning the Second Division by two points over Kilmarnock. However, their time in the top flight was cut short by a league restructure in 1974/75, when they missed out on staying in the top league, now the Premier Division, by one position.

That season of 1974/75 was good in one way for Airdrieonians as they reached the Scottish Cup Final for the first time in 50 years. After entering the competition in the third round, they went past Morton, Falkirk and Arbroath in their run, before facing rivals Motherwell in the semi-final. After a 1-1 draw in front of 20,000 spectators, the tie went to a replay, where Airdrieonians scored the only goal to secure their place in the final. In the final, against all-conquering Celtic, Airdrieonians held their own before going down 3-1 to the otherwise dominant Old Firm team.

Despite reaching the Scottish Cup Final in 1975, Airdrieonians struggled to get into the promotion fight in the

First Division. In 1979/80, they had a surprise turn in form and pushed up to the top end of the league and finished in second place, missing out on the title by just two points, but clear of third place by seven points. However, after just two seasons in the Premier Division, they were relegated again. This time it was becoming clear that the clubs in the top flight had a lot more money and the financial gap between the top flight and lower leagues was getting bigger.

As the 1980s wore on, Airdrieonians became known as a stable First Division team and were never at risk of relegation. Then, in 1989, former Dundee United coach Jimmy Bone took over as manager. In his first season, Airdrieonians finished in second place, four points from promotion, which was followed by another second-place finish, this time gaining promotion after a rule change reopened the promotion and relegation to being two teams instead of just one.

When the club was promoted in the summer of 1991 it was shocked by the resignation of Bone, who had received a job offer from Zambian team Power Dynamos FC, where he went on to win the African Cup Winners' Cup and the Zambian league title. However, Airdrieonians didn't stress for long as pulled off something of a coup when they brought in legendary Hearts manager Alex MacDonald, who would remain at the club for the rest of the decade.

During his first season he took the club to their third Scottish Cup Final. After getting past both Stranraer and Huntly in the early rounds, Airdrieonians travelled to Easter Road and beat Hibs 2-0 to secure a semi-final against MacDonald's former team Hearts. The first match ended 0-0, taking the tense tie to a replay, which was played in front of just 10,000 fans. This also ended level, at 1-1, but Airdrieonians won 4-2 on penalties.

Airdrieonians were through to the final to face a Rangers team that was in the middle of its nine-in-a-row run of league titles. The final was very much a match of two halves. In the first half, Mark Hateley and Ally McCoist scored to make the second half appear somewhat comfortable for Rangers. However, Airdrieonians pushed them, and in the 81st minute Andy Smith scored to halve the deficit, but they couldn't find a second goal and Rangers won the Scottish Cup to make it a domestic treble.

Having reached that final, Airdrieonians qualified for the Cup Winners' Cup, as Rangers had entered the European Cup as league champions. In the first round, Airdrieonians were drawn against Sparta Prague, losing the first leg 1-0 at home then the second 2-1. That disappointment laid the groundwork for a relatively poor season overall, with the team winning just six times all season. This poor record led to them being relegated at the end of the season after finishing bottom.

While their performances on the pitch were indifferent, off it, things were becoming difficult. Following on from a change in the law, clubs in the top leagues throughout the UK were starting to be need all-seater stadiums. This was an issue for most clubs in Scotland and a lot of older grounds would close during this period or larger building works would take place to bring the stadiums up to the required modern standards.

Airdrieonians were no different. Their ground, Broomfield Park, was one of the classics in Scotland. Its tight ground with stands close to the pitch made the atmosphere hostile and daunting, so much so that most clubs disliked travelling there. As well as its claustrophobic atmosphere the ground felt old. Its iconic corner pavilion was built in 1907 and its main stand was from the 1920s, paid for by the money from the club's Scottish Cup victory.

By 1994 it was becoming clear that if Airdrieonians wanted to be a top-tier team again, they would need a stadium that matched up to the required standard. To achieve that at Broomfield Park, it was becoming more and more apparent, would cost more money than to simply build a new stadium. So, sadly, in the summer of 1994, the ground was sold to supermarket company Safeway.

Airdrieonians played their final match at Broomfield Park in May 1994. After the sale of the ground, they applied for planning permission to build a new 10,000-seater ground in Airdrie. While this was in the works, they played at the newly built Broadwood Stadium in nearby Cumbernauld, ground-sharing with Clyde FC.

Playing in Cumbernauld for 1994/95, Airdrieonians finished fourth in the league, some seven points from the promotion play-off place. However, in the Scottish Cup they had a very good season, reaching the final for the second time in three seasons.

Again with relative ease, they had got through to the quarter-final, where they beat Raith Rovers 4-1, reaching a semi-final against Hearts. Thanks to a strike from Steve Cooper on the half-hour mark, they made it past manager MacDonald's former team again and were in the final, this time against Celtic.

The 1995 Scottish Cup Final was a vitally important one for Celtic. They hadn't won a trophy in six years and had only just come through their own financial disasters, having been saved at the 11th hour by Fergus McCann. Going into the final, First Division Airdrieonians weren't given a hope, even with Celtic's troubles. In the match, watched by 35,000 spectators, Celtic took the lead in the ninth minute thanks to a header from Pierre van Hooijdonk. Airdrieonians put in a fantastic performance for the rest of the match and came close to equalising on a few occasions, but ultimately Celtic held out and won Tommy Burns's only trophy as their manager.

Despite the disappointment of losing another Scottish Cup Final, Airdrieonians did win the Scottish Challenge Cup, beating Dundee 3-2 in extra time. Soon, though, they drifted away, and in 1995/96 narrowly avoided relegation to the third tier for the first time. However, the following season saw them fighting at the other end of the table, finishing in the play-off place for promotion to the top flight, but losing to Hibernian 5-2 on aggregate.

Off the pitch things weren't so good. Constant delays with planning permission for a new ground and low attendances after being moved to Cumbernauld for four years had pushed the club's finances to a dangerously low point. Finally, in 1998, they moved into the 10,000-seater Excelsior Stadium in Airdrie. However, this didn't provide the financial boost they had hoped for. Attendances were around 2,000, down from 6,000 prior to the move, caused in part by the time they had been away, and also by the football under Alex MacDonald. By the end of the first season back in the new stadium, the manager was sacked.

MacDonald was replaced by former Hearts and Airdrieonians player Gary Mackay, but by the time he took over, the financial issues were huge. The club had countless debts from the stadium move and numerous creditors were requesting payment. This was then compounded by the death of the final director of the club, Joey Rowan, who had taken huge personal losses to keep the club alive and kicking. However, Rowan's death left the club increasingly vulnerable to its creditors.

After coasting along for the rest of 1999, events took a turn for the worse in the new millennium. In February 2000, things came to a head when Rangers chairman David Murray brought a court case forward to have Airdrieonians' revenue seized in lieu of payment to one of his companies. This, along with pressure for payment from both North Lanarkshire Council and the company that built the ground, Barr Construction, who were owned by Ayr United chairman Bill Barr, meant that liquidators were put in charge of running the club.

At the end of July 2000, most of the playing staff were released from their contracts in an attempt to save the club money. Then in June announcements came out that former Scotland international and Aberdeen and Barcelona star Stevie Archibald had put a bid in to buy the club. In July, Gary Mackay was sacked and replaced by Archibald.

Archibald had an agreement in place to take over as long as he paid fees to the liquidators to prevent the club folding. He brought in several European players, including David Fernández, Jesus Sanjuán, Antonio Calderón and Javier Sánchez Broto. These players became instant heroes and

A late 19th century football match between Celtic and Rangers at Cathkin Park, home of Third Lanark

Cathkin Park, Glasgow. Former ground of Third Lanark

Scottish Cup Final – Rangers vs Airdrieonians. Nigel Spackman of Rangers outjumps Alan Lawrence of Airdrieonians in the 1992 Cup Final

*Skol Cup quarter-final –
Airdrieonians vs Celtic at Broomfield
Park. Tony Cascarino battles for the
ball with Airdrieonians keeper*

Scottish League Challenge Cup Final Airdrieonians vs Alloa Athletic

18 April 1987. Premier Division Clydebank v Rangers at Kilbowie Park, Clydebank

18 April 1987. Premier Division Clydebank v Rangers, Kilbowie Park, Clydebank as Ally McCoist scores from the spot

14 April 1990 – Scottish Cup semi-final. Clydebank vs Celtic. Celtic's Pat Bonner and Chris Morris and Clydebank's Sean Sweeney watch the ball drift past the post.

Gretna FC players prepare for the Tennents Scottish FA Cup Final

Gretna 2 Alloa 1, 25 March 2006. The result confirmed Gretna as Scottish Second Division champions

Scottish FA Cup Final: Hearts v Gretna

10 August 2006. UEFA Cup second qualifying round, first leg, Gretna v Derry City

Renton FC, 1888/89

helped raise attendances at the Excelsior Stadium. The team went on to win the Challenge Cup again, beating Livingston after a penalty shoot-out.

The following season saw the financial issues grow and it became clear after Christmas that Archibald wouldn't have the money needed to prevent the club slipping away. Finally, in March, it was announced that the liquidators had moved away from Archibald as he hadn't been able to keep up with the payments required.

Once Archibald left the club in March 2001, they turned to former Clydebank and Morton boss Ian McCall. In his short time as a manager, McCall had already gained a reputation for achieving results with clubs that in the background weren't in good financial positions. However, when Archibald left Airdrieonians, he was followed by most of the imports that he had brought to the club, which left the team bare, so McCall pulled off a minor miracle by saving the club from relegation that season.

The 2001/02 season was one of major contrasts. On the pitch, McCall built a team that challenged for the title, losing out to Partick Thistle in promotion to the top flight and retaining the Scottish Challenge Cup, defeating Alloa Athletic 2-1 in the final. Off the pitch, though, things weren't so good. After Archibald left, no one came forward to take the club on, as the debts were far too high for anyone to have much chance of making even a penny back on it.

Finally, in March 2002, it became clear that Airdrieonians wouldn't be trading once the season came to an end. This was the turning point, as the team's form slipped, but they still managed to finish in second. Their last match was on 27 April 2002 away to Ayr United. The match was tense, with the Airdrieonians fans making Ayr United chairman Bill Barr fully aware that they blamed him for the current situation their club found itself in. As the match wore on, the crowd invaded the pitch several times before the referee brought the match to an end when fans invaded again and broke a crossbar.

On 1 May 2002 Airdrieonians was legally folded, ending 124 years of history and a Scottish Cup to their name. When they folded, their debts stood at nearly £3m. This was always going to be too much for anyone to save the club.

A consortium was put together to save football in Airdrie and a new club was formed, named Airdrie United, with the hope of playing in the SFL at the Excelsior Stadium. Their bid was backed by North Lanarkshire Council and, at the AGM that summer, Airdrie United were the favourites to take the place of Airdrieonians in the SFL.

It therefore came as a shock to the new club when the SFL voted for Gretna FC to take the vacated place. Unperturbed by this development, the consortium approached the by then homeless, and pretty much penniless and mostly supporter-less, Clydebank to take over the club. Clydebank, who were in the Second Division, had been homeless since 1996 and were running out of money at double-quick pace, as its supporters had to travel to Greenock for home matches. The consortium from Airdrie outbid the United Clydebank Supporters to purchase the club's assets from the administrators of Clydebank. Finally, in the summer of 2002, the SFA and SFL allowed the Airdrie consortium to move Clydebank to

Airdrie, and a few weeks later to rename the club Airdrie United. So, by the start of the 2002/03 season, Airdrie United took the place of Clydebank in the Second Division (third tier) of Scottish football.

They soon set up as a solid lower-league team and have been viewed by most as a continuation of the old Airdrieonians Football Club. This has subsequently been reinforced by the fact that in late 2012 Airdrie applied to change its name to Airdrieonians Football Club. This was eventually put to a vote and, in June 2013, they officially changed their name and received permission to use the original club's crest as well. The club has come a long way since 2002, when the original Airdrieonians became the first club to fold in the SFL since Third Lanark in 1967.

Leith Athletic

THE AREA of Leith in Edinburgh is famous for its historic port and proud history of being its own separate burgh until the 1920s. It was a stronghold of industry, with many finding a home in the versatile area, including a glassworks, a soap manufacturer, countless whisky and wine warehouses, a drinks production company, a whaling company, a leadworks, as well as the standard things you expect to see in a port of the size of Leith, namely shipbuilding, fishing and a commercial port.

The area of Leith was well versed in having football teams within its boundaries by the mid-1880s. However, many, as was common at the time, struggled to get past their infancy. So, it came as no surprise that on the formation of Leith Athletic Football Club in 1887 few followed the team, as it was expected to last just a few years before fading away. The reason for this was simple: in Edinburgh at the time, Hibernian had just won the Scottish Cup, Hearts from the Gorgie area of the city were a force and St Bernard's from the Silvermills area were also putting in strong Scottish Cup performances. The issue faced by Leith Athletic was that

Hibernian were also based in Leith, and with the area's large Irish contingent plus the success on the pitch that Hibs were having, the small burgh of Leith was a difficult location to launch a new club.

However, against the odds they managed to survive their infancy and began to build a small but loyal following during their early years. Their first appearance in the Scottish Cup was in 1887 when they were beaten 4-1 by Bo'ness. Over the next few years, Leith continued to sporadically appear in the Scottish Cup but were mainly involved in local cup competitions.

Leith Athletic weren't invited to the meeting where the SFL was formed in March 1890. However, they proved they were going to become a force when they made it through to the quarter-final of the Scottish Cup. They wouldn't be out of league football for long, as in the summer of 1891 at the SFL AGM, Leith were voted in to replace the financially struggling Cowlairs, achieving more votes than rivals Hibernian and St Bernard's. They then went on to finish fourth in that first season, one point ahead of Rangers, but some nine points behind third-placed Hearts.

However, their first spell in the top flight was short and sweet. After their first season, they recorded a sixth-place finish followed by two ninth places. Finally, at the end of 1894/95, they were voted out of the league at the expense of local rivals Hibernian.

After Leith's brief spell in the top flight, from 1895/96 they spent 20 years in the Second Division, not just due to poor league positions, but rather to geography. Their biggest issue was that on every occasion that they went into the ballot for promotion it was unsuccessful because the other Edinburgh clubs didn't want them in the top flight. Hearts and Hibernian voted against Leith Athletic every time, an issue that continued until the creation of automatic promotion and relegation in 1921. As such, Leith weren't back in the top flight until 1930, despite finishing in the top two of the Second Division seven times, including winning it outright twice. In fact, after being relegated to the Second Division in 1895, they finished second in three of the next four seasons but still failed to be elected to the First Division.

These high finishes came to an end as the century drew to a close as Leith went into a mini-slump. Over the next few seasons, they didn't finish between fourth and eighth, marking their slip down the pecking order.

However, this mini-slump was precisely that. In 1905/06 they won their first major honour when they took the Second Division title. However, this would turn out to be bittersweet. They had lost just three matches all season, finishing three points clear of second-placed Clyde, so they went into that summer's league AGM with confidence that they would achieve their goal of being promoted back to the top flight after a decade in the Second Division. This hope was sadly dashed at the AGM when Leith managed just four votes, none of these from Hearts or Hibs. To compound the unfairness of the voting system, second-placed Clyde and fourth-placed Hamilton Academical, the latter finishing eight points behind Leith, were both promoted instead.

After the high and subsequent disappointment of this title-winning season, Leith slipped into mid-table mediocrity. Sadly, the 1906/07 season would be overshadowed by tragedy.

In early January 1907 they took on Vale of Leven at home when, in a freak accident, the Leith and former Liverpool forward Willie Walker was injured when accidently kicked in the stomach when challenging for the ball. He didn't play the second half and was taken to Edinburgh Royal Infirmary. After a few days he was released and went home, but within days was back in hospital after taking a turn for the worse. Sadly, he died of internal bleeding after an operation. Walker was just 35 years old and had spent 12 years with Leith, either side of a season at Liverpool. The rest of the season was affected by this tragedy and the death of a true club legend, Leith ending up fifth in the league.

The next two seasons were uninspiring, with the team finishing seventh then sixth. As well as these undistinguished performances in the league, the Scottish Cup was equally disappointing, with early-round exits in both seasons. As 1908/09 came to an end, many commentators were suggesting that Leith Athletic's star was beginning to wane and that they were on a downward spiral.

Despite these comments, the 1909/10 season saw Leith proving people wrong. They put a wonderful season together and walked away with their second major honour as joint Second Division champions with Raith Rovers. It was standard at the time for teams that ended the season level on points to have a play-off match to be declared champions; however, that season the league decided not to do this and declared joint champions. This was the time before goal average was considered, unfortunately for Leith, who would have been champions as theirs was superior to Raith's. Then, once again, Leith failed in the election vote for promotion and were not voted into the top flight, even though Raith Rovers were.

After Leith's second league title in five years, they began to drift down the league in the following seasons, finishing fourth, then seventh. However, 1912/13 would be the low point, as with just five wins all season, they finished bottom of the league. Three years after being involved in an election for promotion to the top division, Leith now faced an election vote to retain their league status, and with their record of losing all but one vote in the SFL, their anxiety was understandable when the AGM came around. This time, though, they safely won the election with the highest number of votes. The following season saw a small improvement as they finished in tenth place and safe from another re-election vote.

As uncertainty surrounded Europe, the Second Division of 1914/15 started badly for Leith and they didn't pick up a win in their first few matches; however, they soon pulled some great form together and by the season's end were level with Cowdenbeath and St Bernard's on 37 points at the top of the table. So, the league decided that the three should play off in a round-robin tournament, which saw Cowdenbeath crowned champions, Leith Athletic coming in second and Edinburgh rivals St Bernard's third.

Unfortunately, circumstances outside of football took over and the SFL, under pressure, had to suspend the Second Division in the summer of 1915. Leith, like many, moved into the regionalised leagues, joining the Eastern League. However, by the end of that first season they had pulled out as they were simply unable to provide a team, as the war effort was having a big impact upon the club. When the Second Division didn't return in 1919, Leith held out for another season before applying for membership of the Second Division when it did return in 1921. However, as they hadn't been a part of a league since 1916, they failed to gain entry to the re-formed Second Division, so entered the Western League.

The Western League had been decimated by the re-forming of the Second Division, losing most of its clubs, which is why Leith Athletic, despite being in Edinburgh, took on the extra costs of being the most easterly team in the league. However, they only managed one season in the Western League and, after another failed attempt to get into the SFL, moved into the Eastern League for the 1922/23 season. Another hope for a return to the SFL was dashed in the summer of 1923, when the League created a Third Division. Unfortunately for Leith, they were one of the few clubs not admitted to the new third tier.

With their failure to get into the Third Division in the summer of 1923, Leith moved into the Scottish Football Alliance. After one season, and following a town hall meeting to boost support for the club, they reapplied to the SFL and finally, after four attempts since the end of the war, they were admitted back into the league, in the Third Division.

Their second spell in the SFL started with a closely fought loss to Nithsdale Wanderers, 3-2. After that, they went on to have an extremely respectable season, finishing comfortably in sixth place. The following season, like many Leith Athletic had throughout their history, was bittersweet. They finished second after 29 matches, one point behind Helensburgh, but with a match in hand. However, they would never play that fixture, as the Third Division was called off by the SFL. In the preceding few weeks, Leith had applied for promotion to the Second Division as they were already heading for automatic promotion before the league was called off. However, once again they failed, losing out by one vote to Forfar Athletic.

With no Third Division, Leith were again without a league in the following season, so, following the example of most of the other former Third Division clubs, they re-joined the Scottish Football Alliance. After a successful season, the ambitious club reapplied to join the Second Division in the summer of 1927. This time, at the AGM, they were successful in the election, so were once again a league team.

In August 1927 Leith lined up as a Second Division club for the first time since the league was suspended in 1915. They won their first match back, beating King's Park 4-1 at home. However, this early victory masked the team's deficiencies and, as the season progressed, they soon began to struggle and ended in an unconvincing 13th place. The following season saw a vast improvement as they managed to improve their playing staff and continued to grow, ending in a comfortable fifth place.

The 1929/30 season saw another improvement and they went on to win their third Second Division title. After starting the season indifferently, winning and losing in their first two matches, they went unbeaten until Christmas, then after one defeat went unbeaten again until April. These runs led to them claiming the title and promotion on the final day of the season, finishing ahead of East Fife on goal average.

As Leith re-entered the First Division for the first time in 35 years, there was excitement around the club, but they were odds-on favourites to be sent straight back down to the Second Division. They started 1930/31 nervously, before being sucked into a dogged relegation battle between themselves, Ayr United and local rivals Hibs. With victories over both Hearts and Hibs, Leith saved themselves from relegation, ending the season two points clear of Hibs, who were relegated along with East Fife, who were cut adrift at the bottom. The following season wasn't such a battle – Leith finished stone-cold bottom with just 16 points, having managed just six wins all season and conceding 137 goals.

As that 1931/32 season drew to a close, Leith's fight for safety was handicapped by their perilous financial position. The SFL had placed a demand on clubs that they must pay the visiting team a match guarantee of £100, a figure that for most of the clubs wasn't too much of a challenge; however, for clubs with lower gates, such as Leith Athletic, it had a big impact, as more often than not they would struggle to make £100 even before any expenses were taken out. Finally, in January 1932, Leith took measures to guarantee their own safety and future by cutting many players' wages or releasing most of their higher earners. This, when added to how bad the season had been, pretty much confirmed their relegation back to the Second Division.

After their return to the second tier, Leith continued to slip down the league. The financial damage caused by their brief return to the top flight was still stinging the club hard, as the committee was effectively firefighting the cash flow problem for the next few seasons. Even the Second Division's match guarantee of £50 was making the accounts a bigger headache than they needed to be. In that first season back,

Leith finished in a lowly 16th place, followed by slight improvements to 12th and eighth in the following couple of seasons. However, after the high of finishing eighth, they went on to finish in the bottom half of the league right up until the outbreak of the Second World War in 1939, when after just four matches of the season the league was abandoned.

Once the war had ended and an agreement was made to resume football from 1946, Leith faced several issues to make it feasible for the team to be able to take to the field. Firstly, there was the small issue of not having a home pitch, as their ground of Meadowbank had been taken over by the army and wasn't playable in any way. So, they played nearby at a new ground called New Meadowbank for a single season, before moving back to their old ground, which they renamed Old Meadowbank, from the 1948/49 season. The next issue was putting 11 players out on to the pitch. This was no mean feat as they had gone into a hiatus during the war and hadn't kept the player registrations like many other clubs had. However, it wasn't all bad as they had lost their ground early in the war to the Ministry of Defence, so hadn't had any expenses for nearly seven years. This meant that for the first time since 1930, the club's finances were very respectable.

When the SFL returned in 1946, the leagues were renamed Divisions A, B and C, and for the 1946/47 season Leith were annoyed at being put into the C Division, as they felt it was a relegation without reason. However, they played well and ended the season in third place. Fortunately, the B Division then had its numbers increased and Leith were voted into it for 1947/48. However, their time back in the second tier was extremely short-lived. They were critically underprepared for the new level and never kicked on. Despite being back at their old home, they struggled from the get-go, ending the season with just six wins and finishing bottom, three points from safety. In addition, as the season wore on, attendances were low, with an average of just 550 at matches.

Leith therefore returned to the C Division for 1948/49 and put up a very good fight, coming second but not gaining promotion because the league was again being restructured and only the champions were promoted. The 1949/50 restructure meant that several reserve teams joined the C Division and, as such, it was split on east and west lines, with Leith Athletic joining the C North East Division. (It was originally called the South East Division as the one in the west was the South West Division, but as most of the teams were from further up the east coast, North East made more sense.)

Most of the senior clubs in the C Division were upset by the fact that they were being forced to play against other senior clubs' reserve teams. Leith were at the forefront of this protest and spent the next four years fighting for the right to play in the second tier and not having to play against the likes of Dundee United, St Johnstone and Dundee Reserves. During their four seasons in the CNE Division, Leith finished in the bottom three each time, which didn't help their fight to be in the second tier, but their committee at this time were reluctant to pile money into the playing staff when they felt it was degrading to be made to play against other clubs' reserve teams.

Things finally came to a head in the summer of 1953 when the committee at Leith applied to the SFL yet again to request admission of the non-reserve clubs into the B Division.

This was again rejected, so, in July, Leith informed the SFL that they couldn't afford to play against the reserve teams in the C Division as attendances were on some occasions as low as 100 people. Leith then wrote a letter to the SFL informing them that because of the financial issue and the rejection of their application to join the higher league, they wouldn't be fulfilling their fixtures that season. A few days later, the SFL informed Leith that they would be expelled from the league if they didn't complete the season and, on 23 August 1953, Leith were expelled.

After leaving the SFL, Leith went on to play in the Scottish Cup that season, losing to Fraserburgh 5-4 in January 1954. That match sadly turned out to be their last. By early 1955, they had become lost – no league to play in, no registered players and pretty much no fans left to watch the team anymore. Eventually, the management committee concluded that the best thing would be to disband the club. So finally, after nearly 70 years of history, Leith Athletic was disbanded in spring 1955. During their time they had won the Second Division title three times, survived two world wars and the Great Depression, and they were one of a very small number of clubs to survive the SFL's Third Division in the 1920s.

With a great sense of irony, in the months after the club was disbanded, the SFL announced that the C Division would be disbanded as well, and all the non-reserve teams would be promoted back to the second tier. If Leith had held out for two more years, they would have been back in the Second Division. However, there is no guarantee that they would have had the money to survive for those extra two years, but it's one of Scottish football's true 'what if' stories.

When Leith Athletic folded in 1955, no new team took over their name until 1996. The new team then combined with Edinburgh Athletic in 2008 and entered the East of Scotland League, where they have gone on to be successful, and with the reorganisation of Scottish football in the 2010s, they now have a route back to league football.

Clydebank

THE TOWN of Clydebank is directly to the west of the city of Glasgow, in West Dunbartonshire. The town is world famous as a centre of shipbuilding and to be built in Clydebank was seen as a sign of quality. Clydebank grew with the shipbuilding buzz of the late-19th century, and that, plus the Singer sewing machine factory on the edge of the town, saw its population explode.

Football in Clydebank isn't as straightforward as with most other clubs in this book. In fact, the town had three very different clubs playing in the league. Confusingly, two were known simply as Clydebank Football Club and the other was called East Stirlingshire Clydebank Football Club. Not only were there the three teams that featured in the league, but there were also some others. There was another one known as Clydebank Football Club, which was formed in 1888, folding seven years later due to money issues. Then yet another Clydebank Football Club in 1899 that played in the Scottish Cup until 1902, which folded after most of the supporters moved to watching Clydebank Juniors, who were also formed in 1899 and continued at that level until 1964.

Then in 1914 the first club from the town entered the SFL after having been formed earlier that year to have a team in senior football representing Clydebank. At the SFL's 1914 AGM, Clydebank Football Club were voted into the Second Division.

Their time in the league was cut short when, after just one season in the Second Division, it was suspended due to the war. Clydebank then moved to the Western League, which they won in 1916/17. In the summer of 1917, the SFL held a meeting where the teams from the north-east of the country were removed from the First Division due to the travelling restrictions that were in place. As a result, Aberdeen, Dundee and Raith Rovers were all removed from the league, while Clydebank were brought in to make the league numbers even and because of their geographical position.

Clydebank's time in the top flight during the war years was a mixed bag, with finishes in ninth, tenth, fifth and finally 20th. In the summer of 1921, the SFL announced that the Second Division would return, and unfortunately for Clydebank this came during the season that they finished in a relegation place. At the end of the 1921/22 season, they finished bottom of the First Division, having conceded 103 goals in the process.

Following relegation in the summer of 1922, Clydebank entered a period of four seasons when they would yo-yo between the Second and First Divisions. In 1922/23 they finished in second place, allowing them to make an immediate return to the top flight at the first time of asking. This return was short-lived as they ended that season bottom of the league and went straight back down to the second tier. However, they improved and bounced straight back to the top flight after finishing second in the league again.

The 1925/26 season would be the last one for the club in the top flight. They were relegated after finishing some six points from safety. When they returned to the second tier in the summer of 1926 it was hoped that they would make another instant return to the top flight but, after a great start to the campaign, they club fell away and finished in third place, four points from the promotion spot.

This failure would prove over time to be the catalyst that, when combined with the economic downturn and the slowing down of shipbuilding, meant that Clydebank were in desperate need of top-flight football for them to survive. When that didn't happen, their finances became ever more desperate and, at the start of the 1927/28 season, they began selling players hand over fist. In November 1927, they had to sell their final main asset to a dog racing syndicate for £12,000. This money was just enough for them to get to the end of the season in which they finished 14th.

Over the next three seasons, they carried on slipping further down the league, finishing in 16th, 18th and 19th. They were by now in a tailspin of fewer spectators, fewer quality players and less good football, which led to even fewer fans. This circle finally took its toll in 1930/31 when Clydebank finished in the bottom two and faced the uncertainty of a re-election vote. This was an unexpected situation but, much to their surprise, they did get voted back into the league; however, after just one month they gave up and resigned their position.

In the weeks after their resignation, Clydebank were wound up after 15 years of league football in the town. Their ground, Clydeholm Park, was used as a greyhound track right up until 1963 when it was demolished. Senior football didn't return to Clydebank until 1964, but this story starts over 30 miles away at Firs Park in Falkirk, the home of East Stirlingshire Football Club.

In 1957 two brothers took over control of East Stirlingshire FC. They were a solid SFL team but one that had hardly ever challenged outside of the second tier. When Jack and Charlie Steedman took control of the club, they had the dream of making it a solid First Division team. To make this happen they would need average gates of around 5,000, which would be difficult in Falkirk as the town was fairly small and already had the established Falkirk FC as its main team. With this barrier in place the brothers started to look around for a sizeable town with no senior team.

After a short hunt, they approached Clydebank Juniors about a merger and bringing senior football back to Clydebank. Having held meetings at both clubs in April 1964, the two boards agreed to a merger and to become East Stirlingshire Clydebank Football Club, or simply ES Clydebank, and moved to play in Clydebank at Clydebank Juniors' ground of Kilbowie Park.

The footballing authorities were petitioned by East Stirlingshire's former board and supporters about the merger and moving the team from Falkirk to Clydebank. However, neither the SFA nor the SFL had any legal way of stopping the merger. The protesters weren't perturbed and, led by former East Stirlingshire chairman James Middlemass, started to build a legal challenge to the merger through the courts instead.

Meanwhile, on the pitch things were looking good. The team's first home match in 1964/65 attracted a crowd of nearly 5,000 in a League Cup tie against Stenhousemuir. ES Clydebank included Andy Roxburgh, who would go on to be Scotland manager in the 1980s and 90s. For most of the season they challenged for promotion, but as the season wore on they slipped away from the top and by the new year were pretty much out of the challenge.

While the on-pitch situation was looking good, off it things were beginning to move quickly. Led by James Middlemass, a case was brought forward arguing that the transfer of shares to people outside the company was a breach of the club's articles and associations. Despite the Steedmans arguing that it wasn't, Lord Hunter ruled that a case was there to be answered. On 16 March 1965, Lord Hunter heard the case of the transfer of shares. By 26 March, he stated that he had heard enough evidence and, due to the timeframe of the football season, he would make his ruling within six weeks.

By this time it was clear that ES Clydebank wouldn't attain promotion and it was also confirmed that the gate numbers had dropped from 5,000 at the start of the season to an average of less than 600. While the 5,000 was a high, the average for a home league match was around 2,000, but from March the highest attendance was 637, which was lower than it had been in Falkirk. Finally, when the season ended in April 1965, ES Clydebank had fallen to fifth in the league, some ten points from promotion.

A week after the final league match, the club was back in the headlines when on 7 May 1965 it was back at the Court of Session in Edinburgh for Lord Hunter's ruling, which was short and sharp. He ruled that the transfer of shares was invalid and that the merger was nullified. With that ruling the two clubs again became separate entities.

When this was confirmed, East Stirlingshire conducted an EGM and removed both Steedman brothers. James Middlemass was re-elected as chairman; however, the Steedman brothers would remain involved with Clydebank.

The third and final instalment of the Clydebank trilogy was the Clydebank Football Club, officially formed in 1965 in the fallout from the court ruling. Although East Stirlingshire had removed the Steedmans from their boardroom, the brothers were unperturbed and concluded that a town such as Clydebank would be a more suitable place for a successful football team than Falkirk. So, in late May 1965, Clydebank Football Club was formed and immediately applied for a position in the SFL. They won the vote at the summer AGM of the SFL but didn't meet the two-thirds required for a new club to be admitted to the league. This failure led them to compete in the Combined Reserve League for a season, alongside the third teams of most of the top flight clubs. However, it worked, and after a season of establishing themselves, Clydebank were successfully voted into the Second Division of the SFL from season 1966/67.

They made their bow as a league team in the League Cup of 1966/67 against none other than East Stirlingshire. In a tense atmosphere, Clydebank won rather comfortably 3-0 in front of over 2,000 spectators. A few weeks later, Clydebank played their first league match, against Arbroath, losing 3-0. This loss was a sign of how much they would struggle during the season in which they finished in 18th place, level on 24 points with East Stirlingshire.

Over the next few seasons, Clydebank stabilised, with a ninth position and consecutive 13th-place finishes. By 1970/71, they had climbed up to fifth place, with the second-best defensive record in the league. However, this good defensive performance was short-lived as the next couple of seasons saw them drop down the table, first to ninth and then down to 17th, but this low point didn't last long, as in 1973/74 they were back up to tenth.

The league was restructured in 1974/75, moving from two leagues to three. As such, if you finished in the top six, you moved into the new First Division, which would be the second tier. However, if you finished below sixth, you would remain in the Second Division, which was now to be the third tier. As for the top flight, it was renamed the Premier Division.

Clydebank finished in seventh place, meaning they stayed in the Second Division and became a third-tier club. In the summer of 1975 Bill Munro took over as manager, replacing Jack Steedman, and he had an instant impact upon the team. In his first season, they won the Second Division title in a closely fought contest with Raith Rovers. However, they won promotion with relative ease, losing just three matches and going on a four-month unbeaten run.

The next season in the First Division saw Clydebank take the step up completely within their stride, getting off to a good start with six wins and two draws in their opening eight matches of the season. They didn't let this good start slide, despite a bit of a blip, and secured promotion by seven points over Dundee in third, missing out on the title by four points to St Mirren.

As the 1977/78 season started, Clydebank took their place in the Premier Division. This was short-lived, as they were relegated at the end of that first-ever season in the top flight. They won only six matches all season and finished in last place. Most of their wins came after they had been relegated, including beating Jock Stein's Celtic 3-2.

After dropping back into the First Division, Clydebank still had most of their squad from two years prior when they had been promoted to the top flight. In 1978/79 they fought a very close battle with both Dundee and Kilmarnock for the two promotion spots back to the Premier Division. As March 1979 came to an end the three clubs were split on just goal average, but Clydebank were top. It was at that moment that they blinked. They went on to lose to Kilmarnock and slipped to third, finishing on 54 points, level with Kilmarnock but with an inferior goal average and one point behind champions Dundee.

The failure to gain promotion at the first attempt saw Clydebank lose most of their better players, who were picked off by the bigger clubs. As a result, they dropped to mid-table mediocrity for a couple of seasons, finishing ninth and tenth. However, over the next three seasons they returned to the top end of the table, with finishes in fourth, third and fourth again.

In 1984/85, Clydebank succeeded where they had fallen short in the previous few seasons, as they finally gained the promotion they had been hunting for, finishing in second spot. The season, unlike previous promotion seasons, had been very tight, as they finished just two points behind champions Motherwell and three points ahead of third-placed Falkirk.

For Clydebank their time back in the Premier Division wasn't an overly happy one. They finished bottom again, scoring just 29 goals and conceding 77. They were, though, saved from relegation due to a league restructure, which expanded the top flight from ten teams to 12. The following season saw a small improvement on the pitch, but they still finished in the bottom two and were relegated again, having conceded 93 goals this time around.

After relegation, Clydebank found out that they were to be on the wrong side of yet another league restructure. After the one season where the top flight was extended to 12 teams, it was then changed back to ten teams, meaning that the two promotion spots from the First Division to the Premier Division were changed to one promotion spot instead.

Between 1987/88 and 1989/90, Clydebank finished in third place three times and were challenging for promotion on each occasion until the last six weeks of the season. They were beginning to gain a reputation for being poor starters to a campaign and also poor finishers, which was costing them. By the end of 1989/90 they were starting to drift as they finished some ten points away from second place, and their time of challenging at the top seemed to be passing.

The early seasons of the 1990s saw them drop down to mid-table for several seasons, not doing much to hit the headlines, with the exception of being sponsored by pop band Wet Wet Wet, from Clydebank. After a high of finishing fifth, which kept Clydebank in the First Division after another restructure that created four divisions of ten teams in 1993/94, they began to slip again to finishes at the bottom end of the First Division.

By the mid-1990s the club's problems were growing off the pitch rather than on it. The downturn in the 80s plus the town's demise since the closing of most of the shipbuilding yards had a major impact on the overall community's finances. This hit went on to affect the football club as well, with attendances dropping massively to roughly 600 on average. It was becoming more and more difficult to achieve promotion, and staying in the top flight left the club's finances perilous.

Finally, in July 1995, an agreement was reached with a development company to sell Kilbowie Park for £2.3m, depending on planning permission being granted, although to make things complicated this development was strongly opposed by local residents. Delays ensued, which allowed the club to play the 1995/96 season at Kilbowie Park. However, as Clydebank's financial position worsened, the company buying the ground advanced them £600,000, providing them with a surplus for the first time since the 1990s.

The following season saw Clydebank kick off at Boghead in Dumbarton as its new home, some seven miles away from Clydebank. On the pitch it was a terrible season, with the team barely able to put any run of form together, and they finished on 27 points, some 17 points from safety, so were relegated to the Second Division.

It was off the field that issues were becoming more interesting than the club's on-field performances. In late 1996 the Steedman family, who had run the club since 1965, began pushing to sell. This had been rumoured for a while but, finally, in December, it was revealed that a buyer had been found, and in the new year it was announced that Dr John Hall, a Glasgow-born millionaire based in Bermuda, had purchased the club from the Steedmans.

Under the guidance of Ian McCall, Clydebank made an instant return to the First Division and played some fantastic football in the process, going 15 matches without defeat in the process. They ended the 1997/98 season in second place to gain promotion, one point clear of Livingston in third place but only one point behind champions Stranraer.

During this promotion season, a strange off-field incident occurred that left the fans, who were already angry, positively fuming. The old directors of the club, including the Steedman family, formed a company to collect the money from the sale of Kilbowie Park, so when the sale of the old ground finally went through for £2.3m, the old directors claimed £1.7m. The club only ever saw £600,000 of the money, which was the loan given to them a few years previously, which itself was paid off in the sale.

Clydebank's return to the First Division was marred by fans boycotting matches, meaning the gates were usually less than 200, plus there were very strong rumours that the owner was wanting to move the club to play in Dublin, while remaining in the SFL. Fortunately, while the football authorities had done pretty much nothing so far, they did stop this plan coming to fruition as the SFL, SFA and Football Association of Ireland all announced they wouldn't allow the move to take place. On the pitch, the team finished that season in seventh place, quite safely above the drop zone.

The following season saw the club needing to move stadium again, as Dumbarton had sold Boghead. So, Clydebank moved to play their home matches further away, down the other side of the Clyde at Cappielow, home of Greenock Morton, from the 1999/2000 season. The fans' protest had by now been conducted at every home match, and in Clydebank's opener in the League Cup against East Stirlingshire, just 29 paying spectators were there, of which 16 were away fans. Even if you add in the guests at the match, the total attendance was 69, a record low in Britain for a senior league match.

As the new millennium dawned, the club's off-field issues were becoming worse. Attendances were now lower as the protests were starting to take their toll on a club that was already under extreme pressure. On the pitch they ended the season in bottom place with one win, collecting just ten points. This, though, wasn't the most humiliating point of the season; that came a few weeks later when in *The Scotsman* there was an advert saying that they were for sale for just £250,000.

Back in the Second Division, Clydebank performed respectably before falling into mid-table, while off the pitch they were in court, trying to recover the money from the sale of Kilbowie Park. Unfortunately, the court ruled that the old directors had acted legally, which forced the now homeless club into administration.

In 2001/02 they had another new manager in the shape of former Rangers midfielder Derek Ferguson. Given the uncertainty off the pitch, he did amazingly well to take them safely to fifth place in the league.

However, by now, saving the club was becoming more and more unlikely. The administrators were approached on a few occasions but the debts were so high that it would cost a new owner in excess of half a million pounds just to get them back on a level playing field. Then if you add to that the lack of a home ground and nothing in place for a new one in Clydebank, it was going to cost over a million pounds, with little chance of making even a penny back on it.

Things would soon take a somewhat unexpected turn, when in Airdrie, Airdrieonians Football Club were liquidated in May 2002 because of debts from their stadium. In Airdrie, a consortium was set up with the aim of bringing football straight back to the town. After setting up a club called Airdrie United, the consortium applied for membership of the SFL but failed in the vote to Gretna. So, the consortium looked around for a club in the SFL to buy and move them to Airdrie. Clydebank were perfect as they were in administration and homeless and the Airdrie consortium had an ace up its sleeve in the form of having a home ground that could be used against the debts. In July 2002, the consortium had its bid for Clydebank accepted, despite an 11th-hour bid from the Clydebank Supporters' Group.

In July 2002, the SFA and SFL allowed the Airdrie consortium to move the club to Airdrie, as Clydebank didn't have a home. Less than a few weeks later the name of Clydebank was finally removed from league football when the consortium changed the club's name from Clydebank Football Club to Airdrie United Football Club, which later became Airdrieonians Football Club.

The Clydebank Supporters' Group set up a junior team called Clydebank and ground-shared in Drumchapel, before in 2008 sharing with Yoker Athletic. Finally, in 2020, they joined the West of Scotland League with the chance of returning to the SPFL. The club for now will continue to play home matches at Holm Park in Yoker but have plans to return to the town of Clydebank once again.

Dundee Wanderers

DUNDEE WANDERERS FC were formed as a merger of two of the oldest clubs in Dundee in an attempt to have two teams from the city in the SFL. They were formed in 1894 when Wanderers FC merged with Strathmore FC, the oldest club in Dundee.

Strathmore had led a somewhat nomadic life, playing at no fewer than four different grounds. In early 1878 they became the first team in the city to play in the Scottish Cup and in the early 1880s played several spectacular friendlies against teams from both Scotland and England, including Queen's Park, Aston Villa and Sunderland.

Wanderers FC had formed in 1885 after several committee members from Dundee Our Boys FC (founder members of Dundee FC) broke away to form their own club following a disagreement. After changing their name to Johnstone Wanderers FC in 1891 they moved from Morgan Park just off Clepington Road to Clepington Park on Tannadice Street, about half a mile to the west.

Dundee FC were formed in 1893 as a merger of Dundee East End and Dundee Our Boys and were successfully elected to the SFL in 1894. The SFL could see that the appetite for league football in the city was larger than they had originally thought, so when in 1893 it was announced that from the following season there would be a second tier, Dundee Wanderers was formed to play in that league.

However, from the minute the new league was formed, Dundee Wanderers were destined to struggle. In fact, their struggle had started from the very moment they came into existence. Even their name was controversial; initially, when they applied to the SFL, they were called Dundonians. The Glasgow-based SFL was happy with this but Dundee FC argued that they were the oldest team in the city and that Dundonians couldn't use that name because the press had already used that as a nickname for Dundee. Dundonians argued that if the dates of the formation of the clubs were the benchmark for the argument, Dundee should change their name, Strathmore FC being the oldest club in the city.

Surprisingly, this motion held some weight and went to a vote in the SFL, which Dundee only just won. So, Dundee Wanderers FC was finally agreed as the name of the 'new' club. To add to their problems, they decided to stick to the strictly amateur status that both the former clubs had used.

After the merger, Dundee Wanderers lost the lease on Clepington Park, so for the start of their only season in league football they were homeless. Finally, after having to reverse a lot of the opening fixtures of the season, they managed to obtain agreement to play at East Dock Street, the home of Dundee Harp. By December, though, they had arranged to play the rest of the season back at Clepington Park, where they would remain until 1909.

As for the league season, Dundee Wanderers finished ninth out of ten teams in the Second Division, ending the season on just nine points. They finished on the same points told as the renowned Glasgow team Cowlairs, only avoiding bottom spot because of an award of two points because Renton couldn't complete their fixture against them. At the end of the season, Dundee Wanderers were not re-elected to the league and Kilmarnock took their place. However, they did leave their mark on Scottish football by being the team on the wrong end of the biggest win in league football, when in December 1894 they were beaten 15-1 by Airdrieonians.

In the summer of 1895 after failing to be re-elected to the SFL, Dundee Wanderers joined the Northern League and managed to steady themselves, winning the league in 1899/1900. But it was in 1909 that circumstances changed and finally made the demise of the club a certainty. Since the downfall of Dundee Harp in 1894 the large Irish community had had no team that felt like it was one of their own. Then on 24 May 1909 a new club was formed to follow the lines of Hibernian of Edinburgh; however, the new Dundee Hibernian were determined to not have the sectarianism that had ultimately led to the problems at Dundee Harp.

In June 1909 the tenancy of Clepington Park came up for renewal and Dundee Wanderers thought they had come to an agreement. A few days later, though, they were outraged to find out that Dundee Hibernian secretary Pat Reilly had contacted the landlords and offered them better terms, which the landlords accepted, so Dundee Wanderers were homeless again.

However, they decided not to take the underhand action of the new club lying down and one night in June went to their former home and took a few of the items that they had left behind. These items included some kits, balls, the fences enclosing the ground, the shed that included the changing rooms, and the goal posts. They also dismantled the small grandstand. When they left there was nothing more than an open field left for Dundee Hibernian, who, seemingly unbothered by this, played their first match on 19 August in a friendly at the newly renamed Tannadice Park. In 1910, Dundee Hibernian were elected to the SFL and in 1923 changed their name to Dundee United.

Dundee Wanderers, however, spent 1909/10 playing all their matches away from home. By the end of that season they were no closer to having a new home ground, so had to resign from the Northern League. In 1910/11, they club ground-hopped, only playing friendlies and cup ties, but things appeared to be changing when in 1911/12 they managed to get the lease for St Margaret's Park in Lochee. With this in place the club re-joined the Northern League for the 1911/12 season.

However, by the end of that season Dundee Wanderers were deep in debt. Due to the seasons when they had no home ground, they had lost fans to the two league teams from the city. With the rent of the ground higher than their net income from the turnstiles, they resigned from the Northern League in the summer of 1912.

Dundee Wanderers would play only two more matches. Their last senior match was on 7 September 1912 in an 8-0 defeat to Arbroath. A few months later, on 15 March 1913, in the quarter-final of the Forfarshire Cup (having gone through to that stage thanks to a bye), their final match was at Dens Park against a Dundee 'A' team. Wanderers lost 6-1.

At the end of that season, Dundee Wanderers Football Club was wound up. During their time they won the Northern League just once, in 1899/1900, and won the Forfarshire Cup three times, in 1897/98, 1901/02 and 1903/04. Today, nothing can really be seen in the city relating to Dundee Wanderers except for Tannadice Park, which is still the home of Dundee United.

Armadale

ARMADALE IS a small and young town in West Lothian, just west of Bathgate. It was transformed in the late-18th century from a small bit of farmland into a mining town after it was discovered that a large deposit of coal and ironstone was within the immediate area of the old farm. As the 19th century wore on the town became a centre for brickmaking and at the turn of the 20th century it was booming, prior to the years leading up to the First World War.

As Armadale was rapidly growing, football was becoming established as the country's favourite pastime. A few teams played in Armadale during the latter few decades of the 18th century, including the original Armadale Football Club and Armadale Volunteers Football Club, who were made up of members of the local army volunteers of the Royal Scots Volunteer Battalion. These two teams folded in 1894 and 1897, respectively.

It wasn't until 1910 that a new club was formed in the town, when Armadale Football Club was established. They entered the Scottish Football Union initially but moved on at the end of their first season to the Central League, where they finished 11th, but improved the following season by coming fifth. However, the next season was a fantastic one as they won the title comfortably over Dundee. The 1912/13 season ended with Armadale winning a league and cup double, by retaining the Central League and winning the Linlithgowshire Cup.

They remained in the Central League until the First World War, when the SFL suspended the Second Division, which meant that the Central League was split into Eastern and Western Divisions. For Armadale, the Eastern League was a success as they won the Eastern Division Cup and the league title in 1915/16.

After the war, they re-joined the Central League but finished in sixth at the end of the first season. The following campaign saw a small improvement, but it was the summer of 1921 that saw a bigger change. When the SFL re-formed the Second Division, Armadale were one of the Central League clubs to be incorporated into it.

Armadale would go on to spend the next decade in the Second Division. The first season was the pinnacle of their time in the SFL when they finished third, kicking off the campaign by beating St Bernard's 3-0 at home in front of a crowd of just over 4,000 people. They carried on achieving good results, especially at home, and ended the season with 20 wins to their name, but some 15 points behind league leaders Alloa Athletic.

Over the next few seasons, Armadale drifted from their early success, finishing 6th, 11th and 14th. In 1925/26 they finished in 15th place and conceded 101 goals, although they scored 82. The following season they climbed one place but this was a small recovery, as 1927/28 was a terrible one in the league. They managed to gain just eight wins and eight draws, losing the rest, including a whopping 10-0 defeat against Arthurlie in October and a 10-3 defeat to Third Lanark in March. They conceded some 112 goals in 38 matches and faced the uncertainty of a re-election vote. However, they needn't have worried, as they came through the election with relative ease, securing 23 votes, nine more than their nearest challengers.

While their on-field performances were disappointing, it was off the field that worrying signs were really starting to show. By 1928 the world economy was in a terrible state and Scotland was no exception. Unemployment was rife and the political situation was toxic and dangerous, with civil unrest always simmering just under the surface. The mining towns and villages of Scotland were hit very hard during the economic downturn following the First World War and people lost income, which had a direct impact upon the football clubs of these small towns. For Armadale, the average gate had been around 2,750 people, and in the derby matches it was 4,500. However, by 1929, once local rivals Bathgate had left the league, Armadale's home gate had dropped to an average of just 500. This was having a huge impact on their finances, as the league still required the home club to pay a £50 guarantee to the visiting team.

Armadale's performances didn't improve in 1928/29 and they finished bottom of the table, but avoided the re-election vote because both Arthurlie and Bathgate had resigned from the league, meaning two clubs would be voted in and no one voted out. The following season saw good improvement, including a 6-0 victory over Montrose, but it was short-lived, and after the new year Armadale managed just two more wins all season, ending up in 15th place.

By the summer of 1930 Armadale were in a perilous position both on and off the field. On it they were in last place in the league until March 1931, when a run of six wins from the final eight fixtures pulled them up to 18th, enough to avoid a re-election vote. Off the park their finances were just enough to pay the players, but the required guarantee payments to away teams were often paid late. The following season was pretty much from the same script, again finishing 18th in the league.

Armadale entered the 1932/33 season with limited funds and not much hope of achieving a high league finish. By November they were firmly rooted in the bottom two of the table and really struggling to put performances together. However, off the pitch things were looking even worse. In October they faced Stenhousemuir at home and failed to pay the guarantee that day; in fact, it was nearly a week late. Newspapers then started reporting that the club hadn't paid Alloa Athletic their guarantee either, but that Alloa hadn't reported this to the league.

Then in November two major events occurred that affected Armadale more than most clubs. Firstly, Bo'ness were expelled from the league for failure to pay match guarantees. This was a shot across the bows of many clubs in the league, none more so than Armadale. Then, to compound things, on 16 November 1932 the SFL management committee announced that grounds that were allowing dog racing to supplement their meagre gates had to stop the practice immediately. This ruling affected most of the teams in the second tier and for Armadale was the straw that broke the camel's back.

Three days after the SFL ruling, Armadale played host to Raith Rovers and lost 5-1 in front of just 300 spectators. They again failed to make the required guarantee payment and were issued a warning by the league. Their next match was forfeited and, finally, still unable to make the payment to Raith Rovers, Armadale were formally removed from the SFL.

They played one final match, losing 2-0 to Dundee United in the Scottish Cup, and remained in existence for another couple of years, but never kicked a ball in anger. Finally, in 1935, the club was officially wound up after the creditors gave up on trying to obtain the outstanding guarantees.

When Armadale folded they were replaced a year later by Armadale Thistle Junior Football Club, who took over the lease at the club's home ground, Volunteer Park, which they still use to this day. In recent times, Armadale Thistle have joined the East of Scotland League, which means they have a pathway to enter the SPFL.

Edinburgh City

BY THE 1920s all but Queen's Park were professional clubs in Scotland. However, every so often clubs would try to join the SFL while sticking to the rule of being strictly amateur. Most wouldn't get past the vote to get into the league but one that was successful and managed for a short while to keep itself in the league was Edinburgh City Football Club.

Edinburgh City were formed in 1928 as an amateur club but with a lot of ambition. Having gained membership of the SFA not long after forming, they applied to join the SFL in 1931. In the final vote they were up against former league team Nithsdale Wanderers. City won by a massive margin of 25 votes to seven. So, the 1931/32 season saw Edinburgh City start in the Second Division as an amateur team.

Their first season wasn't a success as they finished bottom of the league, eight points adrift of the team above them. They conceded some 146 goals, 42 more than any other team. Part of the problem was that while amateur players played in the league system for Queen's Park, these were the best amateurs and more often than not went on to sign professional forms for other clubs after their time at Queen's. Also, Queen's had some of the best facilities in Scotland and every other weekend the players would be playing at the spectacular Hampden Park. Edinburgh City didn't have these benefits to offer players so, more often than not, they would be stringing together a team of players who weren't capable of getting professional contracts or were using the club to try to show off their talents to the professional teams they came up against.

It would take until 1935/36 for Edinburgh to move off bottom position of the second tier, when they finished in 15th, nine points ahead of bottom team Dumbarton. This was also the first season they conceded fewer than 100 goals. The following season, though, was one of the club's worst; they gained a measly seven points while conceding 120 times. Then in the two seasons prior to the outbreak of the Second World War, they finished in the bottom two. However, they pulled off a great coup when they beat Hibs 3-2 at Easter Road in the Scottish Cup, but they then faced Raith Rovers in the next round and were defeated 9-2.

At the outbreak of the Second World War all league football in Scotland was suspended. As a result, Edinburgh City dropped into the Lothian Amateur League and stayed there for the entirety of the conflict. When the war ended and league football returned in 1946, Edinburgh were placed into the C Division, the third tier of Scottish football, and despite the hiatus during the war, they continued to finish in the bottom two of the league, this time around with the indignity of finishing below no fewer than six reserve teams. By 1949 it was clear that Edinburgh City's future wouldn't be in the senior ranks. So, after 11 seasons they took the decision to move to the junior ranks of Scottish football.

During their 27 years, Edinburgh played at Marine Garden until they were elected to the SFL, when they moved temporarily to Powderhall Stadium, but as this was a multipurpose stadium, the pitch barely met the basic size requirements needed to play football. In 1935 they moved to the slightly more appropriate City Park and spent the rest of their time there until Edinburgh Corporation failed to renew the lease in the summer of 1955, effectively ending the club's time. After five seasons of playing in the Edinburgh and District Junior League, Edinburgh City were homeless, but instead of trying to find a new home, they decided to stop playing football and resigned from the league.

As for the ground, it would go on to be used by a variety of clubs, including Ferranti Thistle, Hibs Reserves, Craigroyston and Spartans, right up until 2009 when it was finally closed.

When Edinburgh City stopped playing football in 1955, they continued to trade as a social club, then in 1966 a new club was formed called Postal United Football Club. In 1986 they made an application to start using the name Edinburgh City, which was approved by the old company. So, from 1986 a new Edinburgh City played football in the Scottish lower leagues and in 2015/16 they gained promotion to the SPFL, where they have played since. The story of Edinburgh City is one of a club that had huge ambition and tried to stick to their principles of being an amateur team. Unfortunately, they struggled to gain the supporter numbers and the players they needed. With Queen's Park getting the best players to play for nothing it was always going to be a challenge for anyone else. Thankfully, though, through the new team, the club's name carries on and is building a new, successful history.

Gretna

TECHNICALLY THERE have been three different clubs called Gretna in history. The first was an amateur team created in the late-19th century and dissolved in the mid-1920s, without ever leaving the amateur leagues. The second was created in 1946 and ended in 2008. Finally there is Gretna 2008, the current team from the town.

Gretna is a small town with a population of under 4,000, right on the border between Scotland and England on the edge of the Solway Firth. Its more famous neighbouring village of Gretna Green is world-renowned as the place for runaway couples to get married.

After the First World War, several local Gretna businessmen, schoolteachers and soldiers met, putting in around £10 each to raise money to get a football club rolling. Chief among them was a former football player turned shopkeeper called James 'Jock' Kerr. Jock was from Annan, a small village around eight miles from Gretna. He had worked as a fitter in the shipyards of Glasgow during the war and had turned out for Queen's Park during this period. He had also played professionally for Blackburn Rovers and Brentford in the 1920s. It was with his invaluable experience that the club started taking its first steps into the footballing world.

In Gretna's first season they played in the Dumfriesshire Junior League and finished a respectable third, playing their home matches at Station Park, just to the north of the village. However, after that first season they bought a patch of land from the Ministry of War for £200 and planned to build a stadium, which would be known as Raydale Park. It was also after that first season that they transferred into the English football system and joined the Carlisle and District League.

To prepare the ground for the new league, Gretna managed to draft in German and Italian prisoners of war to assist the locals. Gretna stayed in this league for 34 years, winning the title 20 times and winning some form of silverware in nearly every season they played. For one season, 1951/52, they played in the Cumberland County League, finishing second. However, the league immediately folded due to the financial pressures it placed on the clubs.

Gretna were doing well financially and in 1958 opened a social club next to the ground. Then in 1963 they bought the land around the ground, and in 1970 opened another social club. Then in 1973 a Sunday market was started to help raise more money. In 1980 the market became permanent and still continues to this day.

The next league change for Gretna came in 1982 when the Northern Premier League created a second tier. This was the tenth tier of English football, although it wasn't until 1991 that a full pyramid system as we know it today came into existence.

It was in 1983, though, that Gretna became the first Scottish team in nearly a century to play in the FA Cup. They won the match 3-1 against Consett. While this history was being made, they spent £100,000 on upgrading Raydale Park, which included floodlights, a new grandstand and changing rooms, as well as in 1984 creating a new constitution, the main intention of which was the growth of football in the Gretna area, as well as helping to raise money for charity.

On 21 December 1988 Pan Am Flight 103 was blown up over the Scottish town of Lockerbie, which is only around 20 miles north of Gretna. The Lockerbie bombing cost the lives of 281 people, 11 from the town. All the people of the area tried their best to raise money for those affected by this awful incident, including Queen of the South from Dumfries playing Sir Alex Ferguson's Manchester United on 1 March 1989. Also, Gretna played a Glasgow Rangers XI, defeating them 2-1 in front of a sell-out 2,000 fans.

It was in November 1990 that Gretna became the first Scottish team since Rangers in 1887 to get through to the FA Cup first round proper, in which they held Rochdale to a score draw at Raydale Park, before being beaten 3-1 in the replay. While achieving these feats Gretna also won the Northern Premier League Division One in 1991. When the pyramid system was introduced later that year, Gretna won the league again and gained promotion. In 1993 they made their final appearance in the FA Cup first round proper, losing a tight match 3-2 against Bolton Wanderers. It was around this time that they made the decision that their future was in Scotland, as the higher they went in the English league pyramid, the more money it was costing in travel.

The opportunity to join the Scottish league in 1993 came about due to a restructure of the leagues, which left space for two teams to join. After Gretna manager Mike McCartney had spent many hours single-handedly labouring around the ground to get it up to standard, he was devastated when the league elected Inverness Caledonian Thistle and Ross County. Normally this would be a once in a blue moon event; however, in 1999 another chance arose for two clubs to join the league, but this time it was Peterhead and Elgin City who got the vote. However, Gretna were given hope when it was pointed out to them that it had been a closely fought contest.

By 1999, though, the club's finances had started to come into question and the chairman Ron McGregor had to pay the players' wages out of his own pocket to get them to the end of the season. By the turn of 2000 Mike McCartney was sacked and replaced by Paddy Lowery, who himself was replaced in November 2000 by Rowan Alexander, who had grown up in Annan and had played for Queen of the South for more than eight years.

Alexander would remain manager of Gretna almost until the end. It was during his period that possibly the most amazing and outright remarkable story of not just Scottish football but possibly British football occurred. In 2001 Gretna's annual wage bill was roughly £20,000. Much of that money came from the Sunday market, which would bring in around £8,000 a year, while the social club brought in around £1,000 a month, which was much higher than the gate receipts, as on average only 200 people would come out to watch the team play.

The club was pushing ever harder to join the Scottish league as the costs of travelling around England were becoming even higher. This keenness attracted some criticism when Greenock Morton were given only one month to sort the club out or face being expelled from the league. The Gretna secretary Ian Armour was quoted in the press as saying that there didn't need to be any further debate about who should take Morton's place if they couldn't prove they were capable of saving themselves. He did quickly backtrack, stating that Gretna didn't want to appear as vultures.

Morton would survive but Gretna didn't need to wait long for their chance to come back round. On 1 May 2002 Airdrieonians were liquidated, owing over £2.5m to creditors. With this, the SFL gave notice that a place had become open and clubs could apply to get into the league, but they only had until 18 June 2002 to get their package ready and the matches would start six weeks after that date. So, immediately, Gretna and a few other clubs swung into action.

Seven clubs presented their case to 27 chairmen from clubs within the league. Three were favourites: Gretna, Gala Fairydean and Airdrie United, a club run by the same chairman as the now liquidated Airdrieonians and which hadn't ever kicked a ball. The others bidding were Cove Rangers, Huntly, Edinburgh City and Preston Athletic. Gretna were favourites beforehand; however, with Airdrie United coming into the picture, and with their chairman having operated in the league before and knowing all the chairmen in the room, it soon became clear that he held a good hand. Not only had Airdrie United never kicked a ball in anger, they didn't have a ground to start with, but this was soon fixed when North Lanarkshire Council, who were owed money from the original club, was happy to waive this to keep football in the town.

The first vote resulted in a tie between Gretna and Airdrie, but once the two chairmen went through again and Ron McGregor was able to confirm the figures, Gretna were voted into the SFL and a new chapter for the club would soon start. Not, though, without them receiving some misplaced abuse at stopping a club (which even the chairman of Airdrie had stated was a new club) with history in the league staying in the league.

As mentioned previously, Airdrie United would get into the league as well, albeit through somewhat unorthodox means when they bought out Clydebank in 2002. Airdrie's new kit and badge would look very similar to those of the old Airdrieonians. One extra bit of controversy would be that Clydebank played in the First Division and Airdrieonians played in the Second Division, but through the business transaction Airdrie United started as a new club in a league above the one that the old Airdrieonians had finished in. After this, the abuse was aimed rather more accurately at the Airdrie United board.

In the meantime, though, at Gretna the whole club and community went into overdrive to get Raydale Park ready and up to SFL standard. Thankfully, and without too much fanfare, they were ready for their first match as a Scottish League team in a pre-season friendly against Falkirk, in a match that Falkirk won thanks to a strike from Owen Coyle. He and Gretna had history. This was the same Owen Coyle who had scored against them twice in 1993 when Bolton beat them 3-2 in the FA Cup; the same Owen Coyle who had to leave Airdrieonians because Gretna took the place in the league. In the near future, Gretna would stop Coyle enjoying a flying start to management.

At the start of their time in the league system, Gretna's wage budget was roughly £800 a week, of which £100 was Rowan Alexander's wage. So, with this, it would be important to invest in youth. Their first-ever SFL match was against Greenock Morton and, to everyone's surprise, a crowd of over 1,800 people turned out to watch that famous first match. Only 19 seconds into it, Gretna scored, but couldn't hold on and drew 1-1.

Instead of travelling many hours down south, Gretna would now have to go north and it was their first trip north in which they had the best away match any lower-league team could face when they played Queen's Park FC, who up until 2020 played at Hampden Park. Gretna, though, lost 2-1 in the Challenge Cup. However, they won their next three league matches before a losing run that took them down to sixth, a position that they would occupy at the end of the season.

In the cups Gretna did respectably well for a Third Division team, narrowly losing to Queen's Park in the first round of the Challenge Cup, and similarly going out of the first round of the League Cup, losing to East Fife at home 2-1. However, in their first-ever appearance in the Scottish Cup they reached the third round, beating Cove Rangers 3-0 in the second round before losing to First Division Clyde 2-1.

Their sixth-place finish in the league left them 32 points ahead of the team at the bottom of the league and 12 points ahead of the team in seventh, while the average attendance at their matches had more than doubled during the season. As was so common with Gretna, though, more important things were happening off the pitch.

On 13 November 1947, Brooks Mileson was born in Sunderland. The eldest of four children, he grew up on the Pennywell Estate in a deeply Christian household. He was a fun child but, when he was 11 years old, he was playing with friends in a local quarry when he had a horror accident and broke his back. He was told he would never walk again but, in a show of character, in 1967 he came third when representing England in the world cross-country running championships. As soon as he stopped running he is reported as saying, 'I hated running; I just had a point to prove.'

This was a classic rags to riches story. Making his money through insurance and construction companies, throughout his life, Mileson had a love of lower-league football. In 1992 he was the main sponsor of Whitby Town FC and in 1998 he was the sponsor of the Northern League (the league Gretna had been previously playing in). He would remain sponsor of that league until 2008, during which time he put over half a million pounds into it.

By 1998 he had moved to live just outside Carlisle, around ten miles from Gretna. It was reported that when he sold his businesses in 2004 it was for over £45m. In 1999 he had attempted to buy Carlisle United but couldn't come to an agreement on price. It wouldn't be until 2002, though, that the opportunity to buy Carlisle United would finally come to an end, but only after he had gifted their supporters' society over half a million pounds, which allowed them to build a new grandstand. In a strange turn of events he somehow ended up paying a few of Carlisle's better players out of his own pocket.

In August 2000, Mileson became a club owner when he stepped in at Scarborough FC, who were facing a major financial crisis. He would pile over three-quarters of a million pounds into the club, saving them from going bust. A little over eight months later he sold the club, making no profit. They were still in a tight financial situation, but he had at least kept them alive for now. They would finally be liquidated in 2007 and a phoenix club born that was owned by the fans.

When Gretna played Greenock Morton in their first-ever SFL match, in attendance that day was a delegation from the Northern League that Gretna had just left a few weeks before. Part of that delegation was Brooks Mileson, who lived near the ground, although this was his first-ever visit. Soon after that he would be attending regularly and, around December time, he agreed to become the sponsor for the youth programme, paying around £20,000.

Mileson wasn't ever in the best of health. As a result of his childhood accident, his kidneys were badly damaged and he would end up having one removed. He also suffered from ME and is famously rumoured to have survived on a diet of 100 cigarettes a day and Lucozade. He didn't actually take up smoking until he was 48 years old. He never wore suits either; he would often be seen in jeans and knee-length leather coats covered in animal hair. He had a ponytail, and was more often than not seen with a cigarette hanging out of his mouth. He didn't really have the look of a man who had sold his businesses for nearly £50m. As often in life, though, appearances can be somewhat misleading.

By January 2003, Gretna's committee had more and more often been asking Mileson for advice on the financial side of the club, and at a board meeting that month they agreed to work 'in parallel' with him. This included moving the company to being limited and the issuing of shares. They appointed directors, a company secretary and a chief executive to manage the club budgets, the youth academy, the upgrading of the ground, income and sponsorship, financial reporting and contracts. Mileson was owner in all but name by this point, but it wasn't until the spring of 2003 when a share issue was launched and he bought 54,600 shares, in comparison with the 1,200 bought by others, that he was the majority shareholder officially.

As their first season in the Scottish league ended, Gretna were in a tight financial situation, but by the time the next season started there was a completely different feeling about the club. Rowan Alexander had become full-time manager during the spring and when the summer came around everyone expected money to be spent. Gretna didn't let anyone down, as they signed players to full-time contracts, while still playing in the basement tier. Most of the players they signed were in the twilight of their careers, but all were coming from a much higher level and could have easily stayed at that level; however, they were swayed by high wages on long deals, which is something that a player over 30 would struggle to get even today.

Gretna started their second season as firm favourites for the title and everyone at Raydale Park believed that this was a special team. This ended prematurely, though, when they got smashed 5-0 at home to First Division Inverness in the Challenge Cup. Despite this, people still believed Gretna would be promoted. However, by October they only had ten points from a potential 24 and were 12 points behind the league leaders. By December they had pulled themselves up to third in the table and Mileson had become more brazen in the public domain about the wage budget they had, which he said was around half a million pounds. In the winter transfer window Gretna had a big player turnover but it wasn't enough, and they ended the season in third, just outside the promotion places.

Gretna's failure to get out the bottom tier came at a heavy price. The first accounts submitted since Mileson had become majority shareholder revealed that he had injected some £741,000 of his own money, plus, with a wage bill that was clearly unsustainable at that level, the club had made a loss of £345,000 for the year ending 31 May 2004.

The losses didn't seem to affect Mileson's dreams for Gretna, though, as he ploughed on with his plans to rebuild Raydale Park. The first plan was to build a 4,000-seater stadium, but this was soon changed to a 6,000-seater, as entry to the SPL required all clubs to have a stadium capacity of that size. The village population was around half that number, so the plan came in for some criticism when this was pointed out. However, Mileson was quick to mention that while in the past clubs had built big stadiums to get to the SPL and regretted it almost straight away as they had gone bust, or nearly bust in both the Airdrie and Clydebank cases, it was his aim to keep pushing to get to the top flight, so it would in the long run be better to be prepared in advance.

Meanwhile, for the second consecutive summer, Gretna spent a lot of money on bringing in another full team of seasoned pros on high wages in the twilight of their careers, although in a change to the previous recruitment policy, they did also bring in several younger players, including 24-year-old striker Kenny Deuchar, who was a fully qualified doctor and spent one day a week working at Wishaw General Hospital. As well as nearly a full new squad, the team in the bottom tier spent a week training in Verona, before a week at an outward-bound centre in the Lake District, one week after Manchester City had been there. The money wasn't just spent on wages; it was also invested in the ground, with another £60,000 being spent on Raydale Park. That figure, though, was less than ten per cent of the wage budget, which stood at a staggering £750,000, higher than about half the teams in the top flight that season.

The next season started well for Gretna but the gate receipts from the average attendance of around 400 people would only raise around £70,000 all season, less than a tenth of the current wage bill. To cover that bill, they would need an average attendance in excess of 4,000. This figure was impossible at Raydale Park, but at the time people didn't seem overly interested in the figures. As long as the team was doing well and the owner was happy to dip into his pocket, no one seemed to be bothered.

Gretna were knocked out of the Challenge Cup by Falkirk, but in the league they had a run of 14 wins, which meant they were top at Christmas, and when the Scottish Cup came round in the new year they were in buoyant mood. The draw was very kind to them when they got SPL team Dundee United at home and they had a temporary stand built for the occasion. The match wasn't easy, though, as it was originally planned for 8 January 2005, but thanks to classic Scottish weather was twice delayed and was finally played on Monday, 17 January. Before the match kicked off, Mileson handed a cheque for £5,000 over to the Arab Trust, the supporters' trust of Dundee United, but on a grim night, United prevailed 4-3 in a match that attracted a record crowd of 3,000 to Raydale Park.

Gretna's storm to the top that season was finally achieved when in March 2005 they became the first club in the UK to gain promotion, although the title itself would have to wait until 9 April 2005, when they beat Stenhousemuir 7-0. The season ended with Gretna having 98 points from a possible 108. Another record that season was Kenny Deuchar's goalscoring tally of 38 league goals in 36 matches, including a record-equalling six hat-tricks in one season, joint with Jimmy Greaves. Overall, Gretna scored 130 goals in the season. As is commonplace, the more matches you win and the more goals you score, the more people attend, and the crowds increased from an average of 418 to 895.

In the next season, Gretna's first in the third tier of Scottish football, they started by giving both manager Rowan Alexander and assistant manager Davie Irons five-year rolling contracts. However, the figures from the annual accounts weren't as cheerful. The club's losses had risen by £1.9m to almost £2.7m. As such, the SFL told Gretna that they could no longer sign players over the age of 21. Mileson was infuriated by this rule and stated he would be consulting a lawyer about it. It seemed as if this was a rule forced upon Gretna by the Scottish footballing establishment in an attempt to curtail their attempts at buying their promotions, although the SFL claimed it was for the club's own safety.

Not to be put off by the SFL banning the signing of over-21s, Gretna spent more money on non-playing staff, bringing in a community and education officer, basically a coach to try to strengthen the community links with the club and to bring more fans into matches, as it was soon realised that at some point in the future the current owner may leave, and while on a high they should bring as many people through the gates as possible. They also brought in a commercial director to assist in getting as much money as possible into the club. While these were off-field appointments, the club with the new rules placed upon them brought in four coaches, three of them ex-players, to run the youth set-up, which had been moved to Rigg College, Penrith, some 30 miles south of Gretna.

During their promotions up the league Gretna had a lot of people who didn't take to the club or the owner, and on a regular basis would predict they would face a terrible fate as soon as the money dried up. It was regularly pointed out by fans and media that the club was living far beyond its means, an accusation that Mileson would openly speak about, saying that he was preparing the club for community ownership.

Mileson's money seemed never-ending when in May 2005 Shamrock Rovers of the League of Ireland owed more than £2.36m to creditors and Mileson sent a close friend to Dublin to try to close the deal. But in the autumn the deal fell through when they couldn't come to an agreement with South Dublin County Council over the tenancy of Tallaght Stadium. He was subsequently linked with other Irish clubs, such as Bray Wanderers, St Patrick's Athletic and Shelbourne. Also, in February 2006 he was linked with buying Northern Irish outfit Glentoran. None of these deals went much further than him declaring an interest in buying and his speaking with fan groups. At the same time, though, he continued to give money to supporters' trusts throughout Scotland and England. It's thought that during his lifetime he gave money to nearly 70 different clubs.

In the summer of 2005 things at Gretna seemed too be good; a documentary crew even followed the team around for the season. More good news came when Mileson's son joined the board and they were told that he would run the club when his father was no longer around. The continued speculation about a new ground wouldn't go away, as it was becoming clearer that Raydale Park simply couldn't be made big enough for the requirements of the SPL.

As for the season itself, not much changed in the team. For the first time there were more outgoings than incomings. On the pitch they were knocked out of both the Challenge Cup and League Cup in the first round, the latter at the hands of SPL team Dunfermline 1-0. In the league things were very good; they had reached the top and never really had much of a challenge. In the winter transfer window, Gretna revamped the team again, spending over £150,000.

It was in the Scottish Cup that season that Gretna achieved fame and ensured that every football fan in Scotland would know who they were. They beat Preston Athletic (6-2) and Cove Rangers (6-1) before the third round, where they played St Johnstone, winning 1-0. Then they faced a Clyde team that had just famously beaten Celtic 2-1 in Roy Keane's Celtic debut. The first match against Clyde was a feisty bore draw and, in the replay, Gretna put them to the sword with a

4-0 win. In the quarter-final against St Mirren, 2,850 people turned out to watch Gretna beat the visitors 1-0 with a single Kenny Deuchar goal, sending them to a national cup semi-final at Hampden Park.

The semi-final was against First Division team Dundee, who were in the midst of financial troubles themselves, and as such Gretna were bookies' favourites to win the tie and go through to the cup final. As much as it was a great achievement for Gretna to get this far in the cup, a lot of the media were very keen to point out that they hadn't actually played an SPL team. No matter, though, Gretna and thousands of their fans travelled up to Glasgow to watch them put three past a poor Dundee team.

The following day, Hearts beat rivals Hibs to face Gretna in the cup final. This meant that if Hearts, who were second in the top flight, could finish in the top three, Gretna would be guaranteed UEFA Cup football the following season, no matter what happened in the cup final.

As cup fever took over at Gretna, they needed to finish the league season off first, and they did so with four wins and two defeats. It was the cup final, though, that everyone was interested in and Mileson was even seen helping out in the club shop selling tickets because of the demand. In the end they took nearly 12,000 people to Hampden Park, an amazing feat for a village with a population of around a third of that number. As well as that, Gretna managed to get the Hugh Trousers Band to re-record a song they had released called, somewhat ironically in hindsight, 'Living the Dream'. It was a song that made it into the top 30 indie chart and is still available to listen to on YouTube.

The final took place on 13 May 2006. Hearts were overwhelming favourites as they had just finished second in the top flight. In a tight affair, Hearts took the lead in the 39th minute, but in the second half Gretna got a lifeline when awarded a penalty in the 75th minute. Although Craig Gordon saved Ryan McGuffie's spot kick, McGuffie slotted home the rebound. That's where the scoring ended, and the match went through extra time and all the way to the lottery of penalties. Gretna were unfortunate to lose, missing two penalties, somewhat saving the blushes of the top-flight team. What it did mean, though, as the ref blew, was that in a couple of months' time Gretna would have both First Division and UEFA Cup football to look forward to.

As was standard by now, Gretna's accounts were looking even more worrying than before. For the year ending 31 May 2006, they were more than £4.95m in debt to Mileson's company, Heartshape Ltd (the company that technically was the major shareholder in the club but very much a one-man band) and a further £400,000 to Mileson directly. To add further nervousness, it was stated in the notes to the accounts that these 'loans' wouldn't be requested before 31 March 2008. So, the club still had nearly two years to rack up debts unless something changed. Mileson, when challenged on these facts, stated that he would continue to put in money in the form of trust funds and through his son if the worst was to happen to him.

One of the biggest issues for the club was the ground itself. Upgrading Raydale Park was proving more and more difficult as the planning permission was always running into problems, with locals not wanting thousands of football fans in the streets every other Saturday and asking why it needed to be so big as the village had fewer people in it. As 2005/06 came closer it became clear that Gretna would need to move ground if, as secretly hoped, they achieved promotion to the top flight; otherwise they would need to ground-share with another club. Mileson always made public the challenges he was facing in getting a new ground built or improving the current one to SPL standards.

The issues relating to the ground were mostly settled that summer and it was believed that if they pushed for promotion the ground would be ready in time. However, some fans were starting to become annoyed with Mileson giving money away, most notably the £600,000 he gave to Carlisle fans, when some Gretna fans were stating that this money could have been used on his own club and improving the ground, which he was always in the media moaning about not being good enough. It was also in this summer that Gretna brought in a director of club development. The man they brought in was Mick Wadsworth, who had been assistant to Sir Bobby Robson at Newcastle and a manager in his own right both in England and abroad, as well as spending some time at the FA.

Wadsworth was a man who famously had been very good at either intentionally or unintentionally annoying the fans at the clubs he worked for. He seemed to the Gretna fans a strange appointment as the club had a manager, so why was he there? He didn't really help himself when he organised his own press release and said in it, 'I'll be using my experience to help in all areas, from the youth team to the first team. I'll be helping Rowan Alexander, Davie Irons and David

Holdsworth to be the best they can be.' The club stuck by the line that the manager would be in charge of all footballing matters. However, many fans were very suspicious of this.

Meanwhile, Gretna would soon be playing their first match as a First Division team, and this summer things were a bit different. They didn't carry out a massive overhaul, instead buying a couple of good young players. For the most part the team looked the same as the one from the cup final a few months earlier.

On 10 August 2006, Gretna's European dream started. They were required to play the match at Motherwell's Fir Park, some 75 miles north, as Raydale didn't meet UEFA's standards. Some 6,000 fans turned out to watch Gretna play Derry City from the League of Ireland, including a large travelling support from across the water. Gretna started well, going up 1-0 in the 12th minute. Soon, though, it went downhill, and they went on to lose 5-1. In the return leg, they played much better to gain a creditable 2-2 draw at the Brandywell.

After the European fun was over, Gretna got back into the groove of league business, and at any ground they visited they were subjected to the same songs on the tannoy of 'Irish Eye', 'Big Spender' and 'Money Money Money', as other clubs aimed small digs at the club that many felt had bought their success. Either way it made no difference as they were 12 points clear of nearest rivals St Johnstone by Christmas. They were, though, knocked out of both cups by Hibs, in the League Cup 6-0 and in the Scottish Cup 3-1.

In the meantime, it was the business in the winter transfer window that worried most fans. A lot of the senior players, including ones who were playing regularly that season, were told they could leave the club if they could find another one to take them, including Kenny Deuchar, who was Gretna's all-time record goalscorer. Also, in January 2007 they ran into a bad patch of form and found themselves having to play St Johnstone at the end of the month, knowing that if they won they would be 14 points clear, but if they lost it was all to play for. They lost 2-1, and more concerning for their faithful fans was a story in the local paper that goalkeeper Alan Main was ready to sign a pre-contract with St Johnstone. While nothing had been confirmed, he had waved to the St Johnstone fans when they chanted his name, which didn't go down well with Gretna fans or management.

At the same time, the cost-cutting continued both on and off the park, with more players being shown the door, while two more members of staff were let go. A week after the St Johnstone defeat, Gretna hosted their nearest rivals Queen of the South and were beaten 3-0. Main's performance in goal was heavily criticised and at the end of the match the manager took an age to meet the press, and he was soaking wet. It was rumoured that there had been a bust-up between manager, Main and Mick Wadsworth. On 5 March 2005, it was confirmed that Main had signed a pre-contract with St Johnstone. Gretna soon suspended him and he would never play for them again. On 6 March even more surprising news came out of the club, when it was announced that Rowan Alexander was on sick leave with an unknown illness and for an unspecified period of time.

While Gretna continued to stutter their way through the league, the hunt for a ground for if they did go up continued, and with what now seemed like the inevitable truth, they announced that should they be promoted they would need to ground-share for at least the first season. With this information now in the public domain, they entered into negotiations with Motherwell about sharing Fir Park, despite it being 75 miles away.

Before this potential travelling needed to be of concern for the fans, the team needed to win the league, and through April they had the opportunity to do this on no less than four occasions but couldn't get over the line. It would go down to the final match of the season, away to Ross County in the Highlands. County needed to win to avoid the drop, while St Johnstone travelled to Hamilton knowing all they had to do was win and hope Gretna dropped points in a match that was far from a dead cert.

Over 600 Gretna fans made the nearly 300-mile trip to the Highlands at the end of April. In a match that was slightly delayed, the teams kicked off in a nervy affair. The league title trophy was sitting in a helicopter halfway between Dingwall and Hamilton to be whisked to the winners at the end of the day. Soon into the first half St Johnstone were 2-0 up, while Gretna went 1-0 down, but just before the break they got back into it and then took control. The half-time scores sat at Hamilton 1 St Johnstone 3, and Ross County 1 Gretna 2. As the second halves progressed, news came through that in Hamilton the score was 2-4, and that's how it ended. But in Dingwall, Ross County drew level, and right to the end of the match it seemed destined to be First Division football for Gretna again next year. But then in the dying seconds James Grady slotted home from close range to put Gretna ahead 3-2 and topping the league. Although County did have a chance after that, it was too late.

The final whistle was blown and the trophy was flown north. Amongst the fans that day was Brooks Mileson, who had ignored doctors' advice on travelling to watch the team win possibly the most dramatic title in history. He had endured a terrible year, in the summer having emergency surgery on a burst intestine and never really fully recovering. But as he held the trophy aloft, everything in the world seemed right.

As soon as the celebrations ended, Gretna had to start preparing for the following season, noting that any chance of playing SPL football wouldn't happen until they had come to an agreement with Motherwell to play there. The SPL gave the club the okay to play matches for one season at Motherwell and, if Gretna stayed up, this may be extended.

The prices for the Gretna fans attending matches jumped massively; a matchday ticket increased from £12 to £20, and up to £24 if it was the Old Firm teams they were playing. A season ticket went from £196 to £355. If you add in approximately £50 in travelling costs, this meant that the attendances would take a hit.

In June, no one really knew what the management situation was, until it was finally announced that Davie Irons would become head coach and Mick Wadsworth would become director of football. After this, it was agreed that Rowan Alexander would end his time at the club.

On the park, as the new season started, claims and counterclaims were fired between the now ex-manager and the club's owners, while in the transfer window the hopes of

Gretna signing big-name players never really happened and they started the season without an experienced goalkeeper. It took until 22 September 2007 for them to achieve their first win, against Dundee United, 2-1. As Gretna entered 2008, they had managed to gain just ten points but the fans hoped that, as with past seasons, the chequebook would come out and Mileson would buy a way to safety. However, to many fans' horror, 14 players were allowed to leave the club and the replacements were all youth players from middle-of-the-road English clubs. The only one to go on to really make a name for himself was Kyle Naughton.

As February started, Gretna were nine points adrift at the bottom of the league. However, on 13 February things took a sad turn when Brooks Mileson was taken into hospital. A few days later, after a defeat to Motherwell, the staff found that they hadn't been paid. Strangely for a senior club, all 60 or so members of staff were paid weekly rather than monthly. The club was very quick to come out and state that it was an oversight. It turned out that the wages weren't paid direct from a club account but from one of Mileson's personal accounts that only he could approve the transaction from. It was only now that people started to realise just how strong his grip was on the club.

Just after this, on 19 February, the vacant Greenock Morton manager's job was taken by a Gretna manager. Many believed that Rowan Alexander, who had been a Morton hero, would soon be announced as manager; however, much to the surprise of nearly everyone, it was Davie Irons who was presented. This left Mick Wadsworth in charge of first-team affairs at Gretna. With the club refusing to rule out going into administration, Irons asked the fans for a bit of understanding as to why he left the club.

It wasn't until 21 February that Mileson was finally released from hospital and promises were made by his family that wages and backpay would be forthcoming over the next few weeks. Soon, though, the money problem was back, and Wadsworth told the BBC that 'Brooks is still ill and the financial lines have been cut at the moment'. Soon after, Gretna played Dundee United on a Thursday night after it had twice been cancelled due to poor weather. The attendance was a terrible 501, a then record low crowd for a top-flight match.

The very next day, staff from Gretna met with an administration company. Despite finally receiving their wages, it was clear that the list of people owed money was huge. First among them was HMRC, owed £350,000. After just over a week, it was decided to put the club into administration in an attempt to buy time and stop the winding-up orders. This choice almost instantly confirmed Gretna's relegation, as the club going into administration meant that they would have ten points deducted straight away. This left them with just six points in the middle of March and no chance of staying up.

The relegation battle wasn't the battle the fans were bothered about. Never mind no SPL football next season, there was a real chance of no football at all. Many clubs had gone into administration before, some with bigger debts, but the difference this time round was that Gretna were a lot smaller than those clubs and couldn't get the fans in enough numbers to help raise the vital funds.

The most important thing was to stop losing money at such a fast rate. With so few coming through the gates, things needed to change and quickly. It soon became clear that Mileson had been bridging the gap personally between the incoming and outgoing money at the club. The administrators made a statement not long after saying that he wouldn't be putting any money into the club in the coming weeks. Theories soon started going around saying that his money had dried up or that his family had effectively hidden the chequebook to try to stop him spending so much money.

It soon became clear that money until the end of the season was going to become even more difficult to find, and in the end it took assistance from the SPL to pay the players' wages through to the end of the season just for Gretna to guarantee that all outstanding fixtures would be played.

Although the SPL was helping by paying these wages, it still didn't help with the logistics of the club, which needed a gift of £30,000 to cover the costs of an away match at Aberdeen. As Gretna struggled, several parties interested in buying the club came forward. However, at the time they were nearly £8m in debt to Mileson's companies. They did start receiving donations from fans and fellow clubs, including £500 from Third Lanark, who were the last Scottish League club to be liquidated in 1967.

As March came to an end, FIFA allowed Gretna players freedom of movement for those under contract to find a new club if they wished, as long as it was done before 31 March 2008. On 26 March, 29 members of staff, including 13 youth players and nine senior players, were given redundancy notices. Included in this number was Brooks Mileson's son Craig.

A few days later in the society next to Raydale Park, the supporters gathered in numbers to discuss the club's predicament and set up an action group. Once relegation was confirmed after a defeat to St Mirren, former manager Davie Irons was asked in a BBC interview, whether his Morton team, if they avoided the drop, would face Gretna next season in the First Division, to which he said, 'I don't think they [Gretna] will survive.' And when pushed about Mileson's unwillingness to put further money into the club, he said, 'I still don't think that Brooks would walk away from Gretna. His illness must be so bad that he can't do anything about the situation, otherwise it's bizarre.'

The action group, with support from Supporters Direct Scotland and local MPs and MSPs, put a plan together to start raising money and, for the worst case scenario, started making preparations to create a phoenix club if required. The first issue was that around £35,000 would need to be raised just to play at Raydale Park and get it back up to standard for the SFL.

On 5 April, Gretna vs Inverness Caledonian Thistle set a record low attendance for a top-flight match in Scotland when just 431 lonely souls turned out to watch Gretna lose 2-1.

The coming weeks would soon reveal the true extent of the debt owed and to whom, which included the non-payment of National Insurance, player and staff wages, HMRC and even TV licences. The most important debt was over half a million pounds owed to HMRC, and even without the Mileson debt, the club still owed £1.9m to other people. The club's assets, which mainly consisted of the football ground, were valued at just £824,000.

On 13 May 2008, two years to the day since Gretna had played Hearts in the cup final amidst an atmosphere that couldn't have been better, that day must have felt more like a lifetime ago as they faced Hearts again. This time there was a subdued and almost funereal feeling around the ground as 1,090 turned out to watch Gretna one last time, and this club of surprises amazingly won 1-0. The team that turned out that day and left a mark on history was Greg Fleming, Rostyn Griffiths, Craig Barr, Gavin Skelton, Abdul Osman, Danny Hall, Steven Hogg, Kyle Naughton, Nicky Deverdics, Rhys Meynell and Brendan McGill. The goal that day was scored by future Hearts player Gavin Skelton.

During this period, the action group had begun taking the steps required to create a new club. The final hopes for Gretna to be saved were all but ended when the SFL announced that they would be relegated to the bottom tier of Scottish football. On 29 May, Gretna travelled to Hampden to try to maintain their status as an SFL team, never mind what division they were to play in. At the meeting, the SFL stated that it would require a bond of £200,000 up front, plus another £100,000 on a new main stand at Raydale Park. The final nail of the coffin was hammered home when the SFL asked the administrator whether he felt confident that Gretna could fulfil all their matches the following season, and with his professional position on the line, he felt unable to say yes.

With this information, the action group decided to put its full efforts into creating a new club in the town. They soon created Gretna 2008 FC and began the difficult process of applying to the East of Scotland League. Thankfully, they were accepted and they made it abundantly clear that this was a new club that had no ties to Brooks Mileson or his family. The first season they had to play in Annan, but after a year they were able to move back to their old home at Raydale Park, where they remain to this day.

There have also been other Gretna connections for Gretna 2008, as Davie Irons has managed them, and in December 2019 they appointed Rowan Alexander as manager. Gretna 2008 currently play in the Lowland League, one tier below the SPFL.

As for Mileson's Gretna, the company and administrators carried on until 8 August 2008 when, finally, the old club's 62 years of history were ended in liquidation. They owed about £2m to different people, not including Mileson himself.

As for Brooks Mileson, no one had heard anything from him for months other than a short phone call to the previous chairman of Gretna in August 2008. Then on 20 August, Carlisle United took him to court to sue him for £88,000 in unpaid sponsorship. He didn't attend court that day; instead, he sent a letter to them stating that he was too ill to attend. A judge ruled he would have ten weeks to prove this was true, and a retrial was set up for 5 November 2008.

Brooks Mileson would never have his day in court. On 3 November he was found unconscious on his own land and would subsequently die from a heart attack in hospital a few hours later. He was 60 years old. After his death, many questions remained and still remain unanswered. However, as condolences flooded in, most pointed out the amount of money and kindness he had shown to clubs throughout the UK. The tributes paid to him were mostly favourable, but the authors of almost all of them felt somewhat awkward when they deemed it their duty to the fans of clubs to need to add in the disappointment of Gretna's collapse, and that he had gone almost into hiding when Gretna needed him most.

For nearly a year no answers were forthcoming, until October 2009 when it was revealed Mileson's fortune had completely gone. His debts were over £8m, and his assets only came to £2.5m. So it transpired that in February 2010 Brooks Mileson was finally declared bankrupt.

As for his legacy, well, to say it's mixed is an understatement. Firstly, no matter what hindsight tells us about the man, he was a philanthropist. He gave money to around 70 clubs and supporters' societies throughout the UK. He took in thousands of animals on his land and cared for them. His character showed great determination in both his personal life and business dealings. One, however, can't ignore the fact that he took control of a club that, no matter the size of the supporter base, had achieved great things before he had taken over and was surviving, even if it was tight. He took the club and put it on life support. For all the great times he gave Gretna fans, and there were many, he was also responsible for the club's demise, and then seemingly disappeared when they needed him most, when he was the reason they were in that situation to start with. From the viewpoint of today, it can be claimed that money simply ran out. Maybe that's the case. It can also be argued that Gretna's rise up the leagues happened far too quickly; even for a multi-millionaire, it was possibly a step too far and too fast. It took until the season in the First Division to bring in someone who these days is commonplace, a director of football.

It's easy to sit back now and put up plain-faced arguments for what could have been done or not done to help save the club. The reality is, though, that a fan base lost its club and, with great dignity, the new club's committee still refuse to be drawn into the blame game, for which they deserve a huge amount of credit, as it would be very easy to be dragged into one. Thankfully, the fans, as so often in these cases, came together and ensured they would have a team to watch on a Saturday afternoon.

West of Scotland Clubs

1. Beith

The small town of Beith is around 20 miles south of Glasgow, deep in the Ayrshire countryside. The historic town had deep connections to smuggling in the 18th century and in more recent times was renowned for its furniture making.

Beith Football Club was formed in 1875 and nicknamed the 'Furniture Makers', after the town's main product. In 1877 the club was a founder member of the Ayrshire Football Association and played in the Scottish Cup until 1883, but then ceased playing until 1888. After the creation of the SFL, they joined the Ayrshire Football League in 1891, before soon leaving it to join the more successful Scottish Football Combination, winning the competition in 1904/05.

When the First World War led to the suspension of the Second Division in 1915, Beith were invited to join the new Western League, where they would remain until 1923 when the league was absorbed by the SFL to form the new Third Division.

Beith's time in the SFL got off to a ropey start when defeated 2-1 by newly relegated East Stirlingshire away from home. Soon, though, they stabilised and ended that first season in a respectable seventh place. The following season was less successful, as they lost half of their matches and ended up in the bottom three. In 1925/26 the league was in a financial disaster zone and Beith were no different. Despite the gate numbers being enough to meet the league's £15 guarantee, it left little extra money for players. When the league was suspended, Beith sat in 12th place, having lost 14 matches by that point.

When Beith lost their league place at the end of the 1925/26 season, they dropped into the Scottish Football Alliance. They would remain there and occasionally appear in the Scottish Cup until the summer of 1938 when the Alliance became strictly a reserve league. At that point the Alliance announced that only Beith and Galston were non-reserve teams in the division and had both been struggling for a number of years.

For Beith this was the final straw. They had been finishing bottom of the Alliance for the last few seasons and it was becoming unsustainable to carry on. Players were reluctant to play against reserve teams and the gate numbers had been dropping as the fans weren't keen on watching their team face a lot of kids from the bigger Scottish clubs. So finally, when the news broke that the Alliance had kicked them out, the committee cut its losses and the club was wound up in 1938.

A few weeks later they re-formed as Beith Juniors Football Club and have continued in this guise ever since. They have had great success in the Scottish Junior Cup and in 2020 joined the West of Scotland League and now have a great chance of one day becoming a member of the SPFL.

2. Dumbarton Harp

Dumbarton is a town with a strong footballing history. Dumbarton Football Club have, after all, won the league title twice and been to multiple Scottish Cup finals. However, in 1894 the town's small Irish contingent formed their own club, following on from the examples of other cities in Scotland, such as Edinburgh, Glasgow and Dundee.

The Irish community in Dumbarton had twice attempted to form a club prior to the success of Dumbarton Harp. The first attempt was in 1885 when they formed Dumbarton Hibernian but they were unable to compete with the nearby success stories of Renton, Vale of Leven and Dumbarton. They folded in 1887 after just two seasons. A few years later another club was formed, this time called Dumbarton Harp, but after just one season they were wound up too. Then in 1894 another Dumbarton Harp was formed.

For most of the club's history they played in the local leagues, sometimes in junior football. In 1908 they entered the Scottish Football Union, competing in it until 1912, during which time they won it in 1910. They had by now twice applied unsuccessfully to enter the SFL, so decided to enter the Scottish Reserve League. In 1915, though, the league was suspended. Dumbarton Harp, along with clubs from the also-suspended Second Division, entered the Western League.

They achieved success in the Western League, including winning it in 1919, and by 1920 were entering the Scottish Cup for the first time. However, they didn't have beginner's luck, and they were defeated by Alloa Athletic in the first round. The following season also saw them bow out at the opening stage when they were defeated 7-0 by the cup holders Partick Thistle.

For the 1923/24 season the SFL introduced the now infamous Third Division. Dumbarton Harp, along with most of the Western League, entered the SFL for the first time. They played their first home match against Clackmannan, losing 3-2 after being two up. That first match was played in front of just 500 spectators, a quarter of the number Dumbarton were attracting. However, Harp's season balanced out after that and they finished in tenth place, comfortably above the feared re-election spots.

The 1924/25 season was a disaster for Harp. By November they were starting to really struggle with cash flow to keep them going week to week. The situation wasn't helped by the fact that in the third tier home clubs had to pay the visitors a £15 guarantee. This in the case of a lot of the clubs in that tier was more than the entire home gate. On 1 November Harp failed to fulfil their fixture against Leith Athletic. This was the first sign of trouble brewing at the club. Through November and December, they were living very much hand to mouth and, finally, the money completely dried up.

On 5 January 1925, Harp played their final match as an SFL club, losing to Dykehead 3-1. They cancelled their next match and the chairman went to the papers to say that unless the league gave the club the money or more fans attended, they would need to pull out of the league as the £15 guarantee was too high, and on a few occasions they had taken less than £7. The finances were then hammered more when poor weather damaged the stadium, making an impossible situation even worse. The league, though, gave them until February to try to save the situation. Sadly, nothing changed, and at an SFL management committee meeting on 4 February 1925 it was decided to expunge the club's record from the books and kick them out of the league.

Dumbarton Harp would soon fold completely. They had spent their entire time at Meadow Park, just to the north of Dumbarton Central train station. The damage done to the ground in the poor weather, plus the limited crowd numbers and the heavy weight of the required guarantee had made it nearly impossible for them to carry on at any high level. When they folded in 1925 they were never replaced by a successor, but the club's name has carried on with a Dumbarton Harp social club and several amateur teams throughout the years. There is even a Celtic Supporters' Club called Dumbarton Harp, but they have had no representation in the leagues. Meadow Park continued as a football ground until the 1950s, when it became part of an industrial estate.

3. Galston

The town of Galston is just outside Kilmarnock and just south of the historic Loudoun Castle. It has a modest population of around 5,000 and is more well-known these days for being the home of the short-lived Loudoun Castle Theme Park.

Galston Football Club was formed in 1891 to play in the Ayrshire Football League. They led a somewhat nomadic league life until the First World War. During their first 25 years they played in the Ayrshire Football League, the Ayrshire Football Combination, the North Ayrshire League, the Scottish Football Combination and the Scottish Football Union, all before settling in the Western League in 1915.

After having settled in this league, it was absorbed into the SFL in 1923, but Galston struggled in the league from the very start, and at the end of their first season finished 13th. The following season saw a mild improvement by climbing to 11th.

It was the 1925/26 season that was the real issue. Even before the season kicked off the clubs within the league were short of money, and Galston were no different. They could rarely meet the £15 guarantee required by the league, so to try to boost attendances Galston reduced entrance fees but were twice warned by the league for charging fees lower than the agreed amount. Eventually, the pressures became too much and on 26 January 1926 the club wrote to the SFL management committee announcing that they were leaving the SFL. They were the first of many to leave but were the first to put their heads above the parapet, which led ultimately to the demise of the Third Division.

After Galston left the league they continued in the local cup competitions until the end of the season, when they retained SFA membership. They played mostly in amateur leagues until 1932, when they re-joined the Scottish Football Alliance, where they remained until 1938 when it became a reserve league.

When this decision was announced, the only two non-reserve clubs, Galston and Beith, both made passionate defensives to retain their position, but their plea was rejected. After another season of playing in just the cups, Galston re-joined the Alliance when it was reorganised. This time they played a mere five matches before the league was suspended for the Second World War.

This time round Galston didn't hunt for a new league, and with a determination to not turn to the junior ranks, they eventually gave up the ghost and folded officially in early 1940. Since that time, the only football within the town has been amateur and youth football, with successful teams in both. Sadly, though, no senior or junior team has come from the town since, with most fans going to Kilmarnock instead.

4. Johnstone

Johnstone is a small town on the very edge of Paisley in Renfrewshire, one that was planned in the late-18th century during the rise of the cotton mills in the town and local area.

Johnstone Football Club was formed in 1878 when football was really taking off in Scotland. They entered the Scottish Cup in 1880 and would remain a fixture in it until 1886, when they lost in the third round to Hurlford.

From 1887 Johnstone fell quiet amid rumours they had folded. The town was still represented, though, as Johnstone Harp FC, a team made up from the town's small Irish community, played in the Scottish Cup.

By 1891, however, Johnstone FC were back, joining the Scottish Football Alliance that season and remaining there until 1897, when they moved to the more localised North Ayrshire League. After just one season they moved again, this time to the Scottish Football Combination, winning it in 1906/07 jointly with Galston. The following season they were runners-up, which prompted their application to the SFL. Unfortunately, they picked up only nine votes and couldn't find the support to get them into the SFL.

After this unsuccessful attempt at getting into the league, Johnstone moved again, this time into the Scottish Football Union. At the end of 1908/09 they again applied and failed to get into the SFL, but were the best-performing of the non-league teams in the vote. It then took a few years for them to decide to reapply to the league. In 1912 the league was extended by two clubs and both Johnstone and Dunfermline Athletic were voted in for the 1912/13 Second Division season.

Johnstone opened their league account by losing 3-1 to Albion Rovers. After this, their season became one of mid-table mediocrity, finishing in a comfortable eighth place. The following season, though, was terrible as they lost all 11 away matches, finishing in 12th and last place, so ending up in a re-election for their league position. Thankfully, they came through the ballot and retained their league status for the following season.

The 1914/15 season was a good one on the pitch for Johnstone, finishing in a league high of seventh. Unfortunately, with the events outside of football taking a turn it was concluded that the Second Division should be suspended, so they entered the Western League along with most of the other clubs from the Second Division.

When in 1921 the SFL brought back the Second Division, it mostly consisted of the clubs from the Western League. The only difference this time was that automatic relegation and promotion were brought in after one year. On Johnstone's readmittance to league football, they carried on where they had left off prior to the war, finishing 11th and 16th in the first two seasons.

In 1923/24 a new dynamic was added to Scottish football when the SFL added the Third Division to the league system, with added automatic promotion and relegation to the Second Division. Johnstone had a good season without ever pushing for promotion, finishing in a very respectable eighth place. However, they were relegated after finishing 19th the following campaign in a very tight relegation battle, just two points adrift of safety.

The next season, 1925/26, was the final one for the Third Division, and when Johnstone entered, the league was in a terrible condition after a spate of clubs resigning and stating that the financial burden was too much. The league was finally called off in April, with Johnstone in 13th place. They then joined the Scottish Football Alliance, but after only one season they left this too.

With the club under growing financial pressure, they didn't enter a league for 1927/28 but did play in the Scottish Cup, losing 12-0 to Cowdenbeath. Within weeks of that defeat Johnstone were wound up, bringing a close to football in the town.

The town of Johnstone would be without a football club for nearly 30 years until 1956, when Johnstone Burgh was created and played in the junior ranks until 2020, when they joined the West of Scotland League.

5. Linthouse

Today, Govan is an area of Glasgow famous for shipbuilding and possibly more famous for Ibrox, the home of Glasgow Rangers. However, during the boom time of the 19th century, Govan was its own town and wouldn't become part of Glasgow until 1912. Between 1800 and 1907, the town's population grew rapidly from a mere 9,000 to over 95,000, due predominantly to the rapid growth in the shipbuilding industry and mills that popped up around the area.

By 1880 there were seven clubs within the Burgh of Govan. Rangers, even by this time, were showing themselves as the dominant team from the town; however, in 1881 another Govan team was formed from a local athletic club and was called Linthouse Football Club, named after the small area of Govan it was formed in, on the edges of Elderslie Park.

Their early years were spent playing other local teams in cup competitions or the occasional glamour friendly. Finally, in 1885 they entered the Scottish Cup for the first time, going out in the first round, 4-1 against Northern. Over the next few seasons, they wouldn't make it past the second round, until 1889/90 when they got through to the fourth round before being defeated by holders Third Lanark 2-0.

By the time the SFL was formed, Linthouse had become a regular in the Scottish Cup and the Glasgow Cup, adding to their prestige. To add to their already growing reputation as Govan's second club, they became a founding member of the Scottish Football Alliance in 1891 and went on to win the league in that first season.

When the SFL announced that it would be creating a Second Division in 1893, it came as a surprise to most people when Linthouse were the only Glasgow-based Alliance club not to gain admission. They would apply consistently over the next three seasons, until finally they were admitted into the second tier for the 1895/96 season.

Given that they had applied on three separate occasions to join the league, their first season was a massive anticlimax. They finished stone-cold bottom. During the season they had attracted crowds of around 2,000, but on the pitch just couldn't match the committee's ambition. By the end of the season they had lost 12 of their 18 matches and were facing re-election. At that summer's AGM they were saved after three rounds of voting and narrowly seeing off the challenge of Wishaw Thistle.

The next couple of seasons saw a great improvement from Linthouse, finishing seventh (it would have been higher, but they had a four-point deduction due to fielding an ineligible player), then a league high of fifth in 1897/98. Unfortunately, despite the appearance of the club being on the up, the supporter numbers were dropping away; from an average of 2,000 when they first entered the league, they were now at around a quarter of that figure.

When Linthouse entered the 1898/99 season they were already slipping and again lost 12 of their 18 matches to face re-election. However, this time they secured their league status with ease. Sadly, though, the following season saw an even worse performance. They lost their opening four matches and ended the season with a measly two victories. This time round they didn't even seek re-election as the club's committee had concluded that they were never going to be able to compete with Rangers for the numbers attending.

In 1900/01, Linthouse didn't enter a league but did get through to the second round of the Scottish Cup after being awarded a walkover because Clydebank forfeited the match, a tactic that Linthouse would copy when they failed to attend their second-round tie against Motherwell. Soon after this, Linthouse closed for good.

They had started off playing at Langlands Park before moving to the purpose-built Govandale Park near Govan Old Parish Church. The ground (which had a record attendance of 10,000 when Linthouse played Celtic in the Glasgow Cup in 1895, losing 7-1) would be used after they folded by Benburb Football Club until 1912, when they also left.

The ground today can't be seen, as Fairfield Shipyard was allowed to extend its site on to the old ground, and eventually housing was built on the rest. However, if you travel to Wanlock Street in Govan, the road runs approximately down the middle of the pitch, but nothing is available to show that the site is the home of a former SFL club.

6. Northern

Northern was in the other side of the Springburn area of Glasgow. Like Cowlairs, they played at Hyde Park and, similarly, they had their foundations in the local engine-building industry. The football club formed in 1874, playing friendlies against other local teams in the north-east of Glasgow.

Northern first entered the Scottish Cup in 1875/76, going out in the second round 5-0 to holders Queen's Park. The following season saw them reach the fourth round, but they were again beaten by Queen's Park, this time 4-0. Over the next dozen seasons Northern would enter the cup but rarely get past the first round. By the end of the 1880s they were gaining a name for being involved in controversial matches rather than victories. For example, in 1889 they were playing

Carfin Shamrock at home, when at the start of the second half, crowd trouble erupted, leading to several Northern players and the referee being injured. When the match was ordered to be replayed, Carfin won 4-3.

In 1891, Northern became a founding member of the Scottish Football Alliance. Their first season earned them a respectable fifth-place finish. However, they then optimistically applied for membership of the SFL but that the AGM came around it was no surprise to anyone when they didn't get a single vote. The following season they finished seventh in the Alliance but, with the advent of the Second Division, they were admitted into the second tier of the SFL.

Northern opened their first season in the SFL with defeat, 6-1 away to Port Glasgow Athletic, while their first home match also ended in defeat, 3-0 at the hands of Clyde. They didn't pick up a point until the end of September, gaining a draw against Hibs, and their first win wasn't until 23 December 1893 in a 2-1 victory over Partick Thistle.

When the season ended Northern had won just three matches all season and finished in ninth, just above the doomed Thistle and facing a re-election vote. Unlike Thistle, who didn't seek re-election, Northern entered the election but were narrowly beaten by Airdrieonians, 19 votes to 18.

When Northern left the league in 1894, they returned to the Scottish Football Alliance, but their slide was already in full flow. Bottom-half finishes in both 1894/95 and 1895/96 led to them beginning to build up debt and spectator numbers were starting to fall away drastically. By the middle of 1896/97, they were struggling to pay for travel to get to matches and eventually, at the turn of the year, they resigned from the Scottish Football Alliance.

The club as a company continued through until the summer of 1897, before finally being wound up. When Northern finally closed it wasn't long before their ground was built upon by the local engine works, and it disappeared into history. As for Springburn, Petershill Juniors was formed in 1897 and have represented the area ever since.

7. Port Glasgow Athletic

Port Glasgow is a small port town immediately east of Greenock. It was originally a small fishing town known as Newark, which in the 18th century was rented by merchants from the city of Glasgow and renamed as Newport Glasgow. But as the century moved on, the town became known simply as Port Glasgow. By the early-19th century the River Clyde had been deepened and rail links made Port Glasgow redundant as a port town for the city. However, the town moved on and became a centre of shipbuilding in Renfrewshire.

A football club formed in 1878 as Broadfield but soon changed their name to Port Glasgow Athletic and moved into the town at Clune Park in 1881. They first entered the Scottish Cup in 1881 and, during their pre-league days, they had a few good runs into the deeper end of the competition. In 1885/86 they reached the fifth round before going out to Third Lanark after two replays, whereas in 1886/87 they made it a step further, getting to the quarter-finals before losing to Vale of Leven.

After the creation of the SFL in 1890, Port Glasgow Athletic became founding members of the Scottish Football

Alliance. After a couple of seasons in the Alliance, they then became a founder member of the SFL's Second Division.

From 1893 onwards, Port Glasgow Athletic spent 18 seasons in the league system. Their first few seasons were a bit of a mix, with their first three ending in sixth-, third- and seventh-place finishes. After an eighth-place finish in 1896/97, they went on a great run of three top-three finishes. On each occasion they applied for election to the top flight but were unsuccessful in the ballots.

After a fifth-place finish in 1900/01, Port Glasgow Athletic had a phenomenal 1901/02, winning the Second Division title, two points ahead of Partick Thistle and six ahead of third-placed Motherwell. However, their time in the top flight wouldn't prove to be too successful on the pitch, as much as the committee worked hard to keep the club safe in the league.

Over their eight seasons in the top flight of Scottish football, Athletic finished in the bottom two on five occasions, surviving the re-election vote four times. In the three seasons that they finished out of the re-election zone, their best finish was ninth in 1903/04. Their major issue was attendance numbers. They had good crowds for a second-tier club but couldn't maintain high enough attendances in the top flight. By the end of the 1900s, they had finished in the bottom two in four out of five seasons. Finally, when they ended in the re-election positions in 1909/10, they took the decision to not apply for re-election and committed themselves to the Second Division. The club by this point was under some financial pressure.

Athletic's first season back in the second tier was terrible. Gates were often as low as 300 and they were rarely able to meet the league's guarantee requirements. By February, they were starting to have problems paying the players, and on 11 February 1911 played their final home league match, a 2-1 loss to Leith Athletic.

By March the club faced the risk of suspension, which finally came about in April. When the SFL's AGM of June 1911 came around, Port Glasgow Athletic announced that they would be leaving the SFL after 18 seasons. They moved into the Scottish Football Union for a season but the money problems never eased, so by the end of 1911/12, they resigned from that league as well.

Finally, within weeks of leaving the Scottish Football Union, the club officially ended due to growing debts and lowering gate numbers. After they folded the junior team, Port Glasgow Athletic Junior Football Club, took over the lease at Clune Park. These days, Port Glasgow Athletic are back as an amateur club, whereas Port Glasgow Athletic Juniors now play in the West of Scotland League.

8. Thistle

Today, if you visit the Oatlands area of Glasgow, there is little to show how the area used to look, let alone its reputation. Since the 1990s, both the Oatlands and the Gorbals have been going through an expensive regeneration, during which the footballing history of the area has gradually been lost. Most went when planning permission was approved for the M74 motorway extension.

This road extension saw the loss of two stadiums in the local area. Rosebery Park in the south of Oatlands had been the home to junior club Shawlands FC from 1918 to 1960, before Glasgow City Council took over the ground. It was home to Glasgow Schools' Football until the 1990s, when it was found to be contaminated with chromium VI. The ground was therefore abandoned until being levelled for the M74 extension at the turn of the century. This same contamination was also found at Lesser Hampden prior to the 2002 Champions League Final and cost some £40,000 to be cleaned up. The other ground lost was the nearby Softcroft Park, which was the home to Rutherglen Glencairn, which at the time was the oldest junior club in Scotland and had stood for well over 100 years. Rutherglen, though, would have a new stadium built just to the south of the motorway.

As for Thistle Football Club, they were formed in 1868 and cemented their place in history for providing the opposition for Queen's Park in the latter's first-ever match. Even though the club played this first match as Thistle in 1868, their early years were somewhat confusing. Their name was reported differently by various publications and, as they didn't enter the Scottish Cup until 1878, they, as with a lot of clubs at the time, played fairly infrequently. When they did play it was predominantly friendlies or local cups. During those early years, they were often referred to as Thistle Football Club, Bridgeton Thistle Football Club or Glasgow Thistle Football Club. This, plus the fact that they didn't really have a stable ground until 1882, made tracking their early years difficult.

Thistle spent their first decade milling around in the local cup competitions and facing friendlies against other Scottish teams, except when facing Aston Villa in 1876 at Glasgow Green. They finally entered the Scottish Cup in 1878, where in moral terms they got through to the fifth round, beating Clyde and Partick Thistle en route, but unfortunately, in the third-round tie against Partick they had fielded an ineligible player and were removed from the competition. Partick Thistle took their place, only to be beaten by Rangers 4-0.

The following season Thistle were knocked out of the cup in the first round, but the next season they legitimately reached the fifth round, before being beaten by Vale of Leven 7-1. They managed the fourth round again the following season but again there was a humiliating defeat, 12-1 this time at the hands of Queen's Park. Over the next few seasons, Thistle didn't make it past the third round but then in 1887/88 they got to the fifth round but were knocked out after a humiliating 9-2 loss to Vale of Leven Wanderers.

When the SFL was formed in 1890 it was of no surprise that Thistle weren't invited. They were, though, invited in 1891 to join the rival Scottish Football Alliance. In that first season of league football they finished bottom of the Alliance, but the next season improved to a comfortable fifth. When in 1893 it was announced that a Second Division of the SFL was to be formed, Thistle, along with all the other Glasgow-based Alliance clubs, were invited to join the second tier of Scottish football.

Their time in league football was disappointing to say the least. After losing their opening match 4-2 at Cowlairs, their first home match was lost 2-1 against Hibernian in front of just 500 spectators. They lost their first derby against Clyde 3-1 in front of a more respectable 2,000 fans but would go on to pick up only two wins all season, beating Greenock Morton 2-1 and Northern 3-0. At the end of the season, they finished bottom, collecting a total of seven points and facing the dreaded re-election vote.

Sadly, Thistle would never get to the AGM for the re-election vote. By the time the season came to an end they were deeply in debt. The league awarded them £118 from a friendly between Sunderland and a Scottish Football League XI but this wasn't enough. On 12 May 1894, Thistle played its last-ever match, a friendly against Clyde at Barrowfield Stadium, drawing 4-4.

The financial issues faced by Thistle were in part due to the constant changing of grounds. They started by playing on various grounds around the Bridgeton and Dalmarnock areas of Glasgow. By 1882 they had set up in Dalmarnock Park; however, by 1884 they had moved to the more appropriate Beechwood Park in Dalmarnock, which would be their home until 1892, when they moved to the south side of the river to Breahead Park. This was originally called Hibernian Park after Glasgow Hibernian (a breakaway club from Celtic FC, when one of Celtic's founders James Quillan fell out with the board because they wouldn't back his calls for Celtic to only allow members that were Catholic or of Irish background) folded and the ground became vacant. Thistle would remain there until they folded in 1894. However, this ground change would be a major contributor to their financial woes, as when they moved, the Rutherglen Bridge that connects Dalmarnock to the Oatlands had closed for refurbishment in 1890 and wouldn't reopen again until 1896. This closure effectively cut the club off from its supporters unless they made an almost three-mile detour to get to the ground.

With the stadium strains, fan numbers being so low and the unrelenting pressure of league football on a small club's finances, the decision was taken to fold Thistle instead of trying to fight on. They resigned in 1894 and wouldn't play again. There was some remaining hope that they would immediately restart the club, but by the turn of the year it was clear that they would struggle, so they finally folded altogether in 1895.

The stadiums Thistle played at have all subsequently been demolished, most having been built over for housing or industry. Breahead Park was absorbed into Richmond Park in 1899 and nothing remains of it today.

The fans came together after the club folded and formed Strathclyde Football Club, named after the street on which Beechwood Park stood. They played in the junior leagues until 1965, but they too folded, although they did win the Scottish Junior Cup on three occasions.

Thistle's history in league football is viewed as poor and almost forgettable. However, they did provide the first opponents for Queen's Park and that alone should be enough to make them more well known. So, although their legacy in league football wasn't significant, playing that match against Queen's Park at least allowed the sport to take off in Scotland.

South of Scotland Clubs

1. Mid-Annandale

Mid-Annandale, like most clubs from the south of Scotland, are a club with a name that doesn't do much to help pinpoint their location. Annandale itself is a historic district in Scotland sandwiched between the English border to the south and Clydesdale to the north. In the modern era it's a part of Dumfries and Galloway. The club was based in the town of Lockerbie, a town that these days is sadly better known as a location of a terrorist attack rather than for its footballing past.

Mid-Annandale Football Club first formed in 1877 and entered the Scottish Cup several times before folding in 1896 due to the financial struggles of trying to get into a league when their location made it difficult.

They re-formed in 1910 under a different name, but after just one season the new club adopted the name Mid-Annandale Football Club. They did very little prior to the First World War, appearing in local cup ties and playing friendlies against other local teams. However, once the war was over, they joined the Southern Counties Football League in 1921/22, winning the league title that first season.

After another successful season in the Southern Counties Football League, Mid-Annandale were one of the few from outside the Western League to be invited to join the SFL Third Division. They willingly accepted the SFL's offer and took their place in the doomed league.

Their time in the league was short-lived. They started well, winning 2-1 away to Peebles but, as the season wore on, their performances plateaued and they finished mid-table, in eighth place. The following season was less successful. They got off to a bad start and never really stemmed the flow of defeats, finishing the season second from bottom. Thankfully, though, their third season was a lot better, but it wouldn't be so for the league. As the league's money ran out and it closed, Mid-Annandale sat comfortably in sixth place.

During its time in the league, Mid-Annandale pulled in crowds of up to 5,000 for the local derby matches against Nithsdale Wanderers, Solway Star and Queen of the South, but other matches would barely draw in a tenth of this number, leading to the club, like many in the Third Division, being unable to meet the £15 guarantee that the league required.

When the Third Division was called off, Mid-Annandale weren't retained by the SFL. Like most of the other clubs that were in the Third Division, they joined the Scottish Football Alliance, but after just one season they helped form the Provincial League. This, though, was their final season in a league, as by March they announced that they were simply unable to continue. Since leaving the SFL, their gate numbers had plummeted and, with the team in freefall on the pitch, the committee felt it had no other choice but to leave the league and just compete in cups for the foreseeable future.

After appearing in the Scottish Cup on a handful of occasions, Mid-Annandale were finally wound up in 1936, having not played in nearly two years. After they folded no football outside of amateur teams was played in the town until 1956, when another new Mid-Annandale Football Club was formed, which in 2003 joined the South of Scotland League, which is a feeder to the Lowland League.

2. Nithsdale Wanderers

Nithsdale Wanderers Football Club were based in the village of Sanquhar on the banks of the River Nith. The village is more famous for its post office, which has been working since 1712 and is thought to be the oldest working post office in the world. Nithsdale Wanderers formed in 1897 and gained their name from the historic district of Nithsdale where the club were based.

When formed, they remained and were successful in local leagues until 1909, when they joined the Scottish Football Combination. They were then joint winners of the league in 1909, before leaving it after two seasons to join the Scottish Football Union, upon the collapse of the Combination. They remained in the Scottish Football Union until the outbreak of the First World War.

Once the war ended, Nithsdale remained in a sort of limbo, playing mostly in cup matches until 1922 when they joined the Western League. After just one season, they then joined the SFL Third Division, along with most of the rest of the Western League clubs.

Unlike most of the clubs that joined the Third Division and have appeared in this book, Nithsdale Wanderers were successful in the league system. In their first season they finished in a respectable sixth place but then the following season was a great one for the team. They won the league title comfortably, three points ahead of local rivals Queen of the South, and their season included a title-clinching 8-0 victory over Montrose.

Thanks to the advent of automatic promotion and relegation, Nithsdale Wanderers entered the Second Division for the 1925/26 season. By doing so, they avoided the imminent closure of the Third Division. They then had a good run in the Second Division that first season, finishing mid-table, 12th out of 20 teams.

However, their second season was nothing shy of a complete disaster. They finished bottom, nine points adrift of safety, and conceded 100 goals in the process. With the demise of the Third Division the season before, they therefore faced a re-election vote instead. Unfortunately for Wanderers, they made one final bit of league history, as in the summer AGM of the SFL, they became the last club to be removed from the league through the re-election process.

For the 1927/28 season, Nithsdale Wanderers joined the Provincial League, but after one season the league collapsed and the club, along with most of the others, moved on to join the Scottish Football Alliance. Over the next few seasons, Wanderers made numerous attempts to regain their league status but on each occasion struggled to gain the needed support from the other clubs.

Throughout the 1930s they played in the Scottish Cup, making appearances until 1947 when they were defeated in the first round by Aberdeen, 5-0. Nithsdale Wanderers finally stopped playing senior football in 1951, when they moved to the junior ranks, staying there until the end of 1963/64, when they folded, due in the most part to a lack of supporter numbers.

After the folding of Nithsdale Wanderers in 1964 it would take until 2001 for a new club to be formed in the town. Some 37 years after Wanderers' demise, this new club entered into the South of Scotland League and have been there ever since.

3. Solway Star

The puzzling name of Solway Star was that of a club from the small historic harbour town of Annan near the border with England. Due to the remoteness of the Solway coast, football took a long time to take hold, and combined with the small population, it was no surprise that it took until 1911 for a club to be created in the town.

Solway Star Football Club formed in 1911, playing on the outskirts of Annan at Kimmeter Green Park. Their early years were spent playing friendlies against the bigger English and Scottish clubs on pre-season tours, or playing in the local cup competitions.

Within a few years, Solway had joined the Southern Counties League for the 1914/15 season. Within months, though, the league was suspended for the duration of the First World War, leaving Solway to play friendlies again until the league was restarted in 1921.

Having played only one part-season in the Southern Counties League, Solway moved on to the much bigger and more successful Western League in 1922/23. Again, though, after just a single season they joined the SFL's Third Division, when the Western League was absorbed into the SFL.

Solway's time in the Third Division was respectable, with two 11th-place finishes either side of a fantastic third-place finish in their second season. That season included remaining undefeated at home and ending level on points with Queen of the South, although behind on goal average.

In 1925/26, when the Third Division was called off, Solway Star were one of the few clubs not under great financial strain. As many others did, they joined the Scottish Football Alliance, but after one season they dropped into the more local Provincial League for 1927/28. Once that season ended they moved on again, this time to the re-formed Southern Counties League, where they stayed until the summer of 1933.

In that summer, Solway were struggling to get enough players to form a team that could consistently play week in, week out in a league system and the demands that it placed upon them. The other issue was a slow decrease in the amount of money the club was taking in. During the First World War, the munitions factory, HM Factory Gretna, was one of the biggest in the country, which at its height in 1917 employed over 17,500 people, two-thirds of whom were women. However, after the war's end the number of people employed by the factories plummeted, which in turn affected the gates of Solway Star, who were the nearest club to the site.

The average gate dropped from around 1,000 people in 1924 to around 150 by the end of the 1932/33 season, so the club took the decision to concentrate on the cups and friendlies, hoping that within a few seasons the demand for league football would return to the town. Sadly, circumstances overtook them. The outset of the Second World War brought a boost to the local population and the club played some big friendlies, but in the downturn after war, they again found themselves struggling, and finally in 1947 they were wound up.

Part of the reason why Solway Star struggled after the war was because a new club, Annan Athletic Football Club, had been formed in 1942 and played in the local leagues during the war. This is something that Solway hadn't done, so when Annan Athletic joined the junior ranks it effectively sealed the fate of Solway Star.

Since 1947 the town of Annan has been represented by Annan Athletic, who performed well in the junior leagues, and finally, in 2008 after the collapse of Gretna FC, they joined the SFL Third Division, which is where they have stayed since.

East of Scotland Clubs

1. Lochgelly United

Lochgelly is a small Fife town of 6,000 people sandwiched near enough halfway between Dunfermline and Kirkcaldy. Like many in the area, it's a classic Fife mining town, which since the 1960s has gradually been on the decline. However, during its heyday around the turn of the century it was a positive place, and even had the nickname of the 'Happy Valley'.

Lochgelly United formed in 1890 from the town's two main teams, Lochgelly Athletic, who themselves were formed in 1886 as a works team for a local mining pit, and Fifeshire Hibernian, who were formed by a group of Irish immigrants in 1889. The new club's early years were spent playing in local cups, until 1895 when they entered the Northern League and the Scottish Cup for the first time. In the league they finished in mid-table, but in the cup they were defeated in the first round by Raith Rovers 5-2 in a replay after the initial result had been challenged by Raith.

After another first-round loss the following season, Lochgelly didn't enter the Scottish Cup again until 1902, and between then and 1905 only got past the first round once, going out in the second round to Celtic.

By the 1905/06 season, they had started on the path of trying to get themselves into the SFL. At that season's AGM they applied for a spot in the Second Division, despite having finished bottom of the Northern League. Unsurprisingly, they didn't get the support required to gain a position in the league.

In 1909 Lochgelly transferred to the more local Central League and remained there, apart from a one-season hiatus to the Eastern League in 1912/13, until finally achieving their goal of getting into the SFL. In the summer of 1914's AGM it was announced that the second tier would be extended to 14 clubs and, after several rounds of ballots, Lochgelly were voted into the league set-up.

However, they got off to a bad start in the 1914/15 season, losing to local rivals Cowdenbeath 4-0, followed up by a 5-1 defeat to St Johnstone. Soon the season would turn into chaos, as players were leaving clubs up and down the land to join the forces. Clubs were struggling to put a team on the pitch and, when the war continued past Christmas and casualty numbers were mounting, it was becoming hard to be a footballer and not have white feathers pressed into your hands. When the season ended in April, Lochgelly were in tenth place.

Soon after the end of the season, though, the league was suspended for the duration of the war. As the teams were split into east and west divisions, Lochgelly joined the Eastern League until 1919, when it re-joined the Central League.

In 1921 the Central League had been absorbed into the SFL and became the new Second Division. From the new season, the re-election vote was removed in favour of automatic promotion and relegation. To compound these new rules, in the first season of the second tier the bottom two teams would drop out of the league and have no hope of winning a re-election vote. Fortunately, Lochgelly managed to stay in the league, finishing 18th, just above the bottom two.

In 1922/23 they managed to equal their league-high finish of tenth but the following season was a disaster. They finished bottom of the league with just four wins out of 38 matches. Thankfully, their league status was saved by the creation of the Third Division that same season.

Lochgelly's first season in the Third Division was a successful one, finishing in fifth place, having won 15 matches. Sadly, the following season wasn't as successful for either the club or the league. By April 1926 the league could no longer financially survive and with a match of the season remaining it was abandoned. Lochgelly finished in ninth place.

Once they had left the SFL, Lochgelly spent a season in the Scottish Alliance Northern Section, but left that to concentrate on cup ties. This plan didn't go well as they went out to Brechin City in 1927/28, Hearts in 1931/32, losing 13-3 at Tynecastle, and finally Kilmarnock in 1932/33, losing 3-1.

Lochgelly were wound up in the summer of 1933. With no league to play in and the success of the other local league teams and the local junior team Lochgelly Albert, it was no surprise when the club folded.

Lochgelly had spent most of its time at Recreation Park in the town, and football would continue being played there for another few seasons before the ground was sold to the local council. Today, if you drive down Timmons Street, you are effectively passing through what was the middle of the ground. Since the club folded there have been no calls for another one, as Lochgelly Albert were already a solid junior club, and are still going today in the lower leagues of Scotland with a chance of one day getting to the SPFL.

Bathgate

The historic town of Bathgate is one of the better known in Scotland. Its historic parish has been on record since the time of King Malcolm IV in the middle of the 12th century. Since the 17th century, though, it has been well known as a mining town, with everything from silver ore to coal and limestone being found in the local area. This rich landscape led to Bathgate becoming extremely prosperous in the mid-19th century.

Football came to the town relatively late compared with other towns in the Central Belt of Scotland. The first reports of a club in Bathgate come from 1878, and over the next 15 years several teams represented the town, but it wasn't until 1893 that Bathgate Football Club were formed and survived the turbulent early years of being a newborn club.

They first entered the Scottish Cup a few years later, in 1897, being defeated in the first round 5-0 by Blantyre. They also entered the cup in 1898, being beaten in the first round again, this time 4-2 at the hands of Cartvale. They then wouldn't enter the Scottish Cup again for another seven seasons.

In the meantime, they kept playing in friendlies and local cups, until they joined the Central Combination League in

1902/03. Having completed that season well, they moved on to the Midland League for 1903/04. By 1909/10 they had moved leagues again, this time to the Central League, staying there until 1915. During their time in the Central League, Bathgate consistently finished well up the table, and they won the Linlithgowshire Cup twice. With these successes in both league and cup, they applied three times to get into the SFL but on each occasion failed to achieve enough votes, although in 1913 they managed to push the voting through to a fourth ballot before being beaten by Johnstone.

Bathgate continued doing well in the Central League until it was brought to a halt by the First World War. In the summer of 1915 they, along with most of the east coast clubs from the now suspended Second Division, came together and formed the Eastern League. Bathgate remained in this league until the war's end and in the summer of 1919 returned to the Central League, remaining in it for only a couple of seasons until 1921, when they joined the renewed SFL Second Division.

Their time in the Second Division was a clear split between very successful and very poor finishes in the league. Up to 1924 they recorded finishes in fifth, fifth and third, respectively. In 1923/24, when they finished in third, they were still some 11 points adrift of the promotion place and, following this, they had a big bounce back to earth the following season when they finished in 16th place, just six points above relegation. The 1925/26 season was even worse, finishing in 19th, having conceded 105 goals in the process. Fortunately for them, the Third Division had collapsed during the season, so they didn't face relegation to the financial mire of that division. Instead, they had to face a re-election vote.

During the summer, Bathgate survived re-election and the following season saw them reach 17th in the league, thus avoiding another re-election vote. However, they entered 1927/28 with money issues but, thanks to some transfer business, they were able to compete, ending the season in 19th place. At the re-election vote, they were runaway leaders and remained in the league set-up.

The season 1928/29 was like the last few had been. Ever since the miners' strike of 1926 the club had seen unstable attendance figures, and as the miners in the local area were striking a lot during these years it made things difficult for the club to be run effectively. Then there was the issue of the directors. Bathgate had several older directors who had been with the club since it was first created, and some who had been in their positions for nearly 35 years were looking to retire. There simply wasn't anyone to take their places, and no matter how much the club tried, they were finding it increasingly difficult to find new people to bring in. This, added to the heavy financial pressure the club faced to maintain its league status, meant the writing was on the wall.

Even before the 1928/29 season kicked off, rumours were rife that Bathgate wouldn't enter the league, even though just weeks before they had survived a re-election vote. They did continue, though, but as the season wore on their money issues were becoming more and more inhibitive to their on-field chances. Finally, in mid-February 1929, it became clear that even getting to the end of the season might be a real challenge, as on 16 February they lost 2-1 to King's Park in front of just 200 people. A week later they travelled to Dumbarton in what turned out to be Bathgate's last SFL match, losing 3-0. In the week after that defeat, Bathgate announced that they would be withdrawing from the SFL. On 12 March 1929, the League Management Committee officially announced that the club would be removed and its record for that season expunged from the official records.

Bathgate, having left the league behind, moved into the more local and less expensive East of Scotland League for 1929/30 and went on to win it in two consecutive seasons. They left this league after the 1931/32 season intending to enter the Edinburgh and District League, but never played a match.

The club itself continued as a company until 1938, but never played a match after 1932. Finally, the last director had the club wound up in October of that year, bringing an end to senior football in Bathgate. They had never managed to sort their finances out properly following on from the early 1920s, and by the mid-1930s the town was in the process of forming a junior team, which they duly did in 1937 when Bathgate Thistle Football Club appeared. They still represent the town to this day and won the Scottish Junior Cup in 2007. In recent years, Bathgate Thistle have become a senior club and now compete in the East of Scotland League, a feeder to the Lowland League.

2. Bo'ness

Bo'ness (originally called Borrowstounness) is these days a conservation town with a historical town centre and harbour area, even with its own steam railway. The town was affected massively by the Industrial Revolution and with its location on the Firth of Forth, the local abundance of fossil fuels and a thriving pottery industry, its importance and value grew rapidly during the 19th century.

Football came to the town originally in the early 1870s, but it wouldn't be until 1882 that a team was officially established. Bo'ness Football Club formed in the summer of 1882 and quickly became an important part of the local footballing community. Two years later they were a founding member of the Linlithgowshire Football Association and the Linlithgowshire County Cup, which they won in that first year. In 1884 they also entered the Scottish Cup for the first time, losing 2-0 away to Hibs.

With the creation of the SFL in 1890 Bo'ness were annoyed at not being invited. So, they took a leaf from the book of other clubs and came together with them to form the Eastern Football Alliance. This league sadly wouldn't even make it to the end of its first season, dogged with money and travel problems from the very start, plus teams choosing to play friendlies over league matches. With a committee that wasn't forceful enough, the Alliance was never destined to last and by March 1892 the endeavour was abandoned.

Having played in a variety of local leagues, Bo'ness joined the Central Combination League for two seasons starting in 1901/02. After this they joined the Midland League from 1903/04. In the 1906/07 season the clubs in the Midland League moved, among those from the Scottish Combination, to form the Scottish Football Union. Within a few seasons of inconsistent results, Bo'ness, along with several clubs from the Northern League, came together to form the Central League in 1909.

Prior to the First World War, Bo'ness finished comfortably in mid-table, not pulling up any trees in the process. In 1915 the league was suspended for the duration of the conflict and when the war ended, it returned, with Bo'ness becoming champions in both 1919/20 and 1920/21.

In 1921 the SFL brought back the old Second Division following its own wartime suspension. The Central League along with the Eastern and Western Leagues were all to lose most of their clubs to the Second Division. Bo'ness were amongst them and proudly took their place in the Second Division for the 1921/22 season.

Their first five seasons in the SFL were respectable upper-mid-table finishes, ending each season between sixth and 12th. The 1926/27 season was their best in league football, although the start was a bit uneasy, but by October 1926 they had gone on a 20-match unbeaten run, ending the season with only five defeats, half the number of any other team.

For 1927/28 Bo'ness entered the top flight of Scottish football for the first time. Their first match in the First Division was a home 2-1 win over Falkirk in front of nearly 10,000 spectators. Their home form was to prove crucial as they lost all six of their opening away matches, whereas at home they had four wins, one draw and one loss. Sadly, even this form wasn't enough. As the season progressed, they would only pick up nine wins and eight draws all season. This meant that they ended the season two points from safety and after just one season were relegated back to the Second Division, but they hadn't disgraced themselves.

Once they re-entered the Second Division, Bo'ness lost most of their players that had performed in the First Division and at the kick-off of the new season only three remained from that previous team. In their first season back in the second tier they ended in tenth place, having won 15 matches, losing 15 and drawing the rest.

Bo'ness struggled the following season as well, ending it in 13th place. However, that wasn't as bad as 1930/31, which saw them finish bottom of the Second Division. They had never been able to replace the players they had lost when they were relegated a few seasons earlier and, to add to this, the economic downturn had a big impact on the number of supporters coming through the turnstiles, to the point where the club had allowed unemployed people through the gate for free after 30 minutes. This practice was stopped, though, after the SFL censored the club for doing so. As the season wore on Bo'ness were really starting to struggle to meet the league's required guarantee and ended up stone-cold bottom in the league, conceding 100 goals in the process.

Surprisingly, they survived re-election and entered the 1931/32 season, which was more successful, finishing safely in 14th. However, financial issues were really starting to bite the club hard. When the 1932/33 season kicked off it was believed by many that they would really struggle. In October they hosted Stenhousemuir and lost 3-2, but that wasn't the main issue. As the home club, they were required by the SFL to pay the visitors a £50 guarantee but they could only muster £10, so they were reported to the SFL.

A few weeks later they faced Brechin City at home and this time paid none of the required guarantee. Within a week, they were ordered to pay the outstanding money to Stenhousemuir and Brechin. Bo'ness protested, as at the Brechin match the gate income was only £7, but these protests fell on deaf ears and the club was expelled from the league. They still played in the Scottish Cup for the season, reaching the second round, where they hosted Dundee at home in front of 3,000 people. They had the gate receipts of £150 seized to pay the money owed to Brechin City and Stenhousemuir.

After the disaster of the 1932/33 season, Bo'ness moved into the local Edinburgh and District League until the Second World War, when the league was suspended. When the war was over, Bo'ness, having continued as a club but not played, faced the issue of trying to rebuild. With hardly any financial backing at all, they took the decision to fold and merge with local junior team Bo'ness Cadora Juniors Football Club to form Bo'ness United Football Club.

The new team continued to play at Bo'ness's former home of Newtown Park and have over the years become one of the strongest junior teams in Scotland, winning the Scottish Junior Cup three times, and in 2018 became a senior club when they entered the East of Scotland League, winning it in 2020 and going into the Lowland League, one step below the SPFL.

3. Broxburn United

Broxburn is a small town 12 miles east of Edinburgh and has its history from the mid-14th century. In more recent times, though, it was better known for the Shell oil industry. The town was a hotbed of football during those early days, with it being home to around seven clubs, including Broxburn

Thistle FC, Broxburn Shamrock and Broxburn Harp, who all played in the Linlithgowshire Cup.

Broxburn Thistle became Broxburn United Football Club in 1883 and grew in stature. In 1891/92, they and Broxburn Shamrock joined the Eastern Football Alliance. However, this league didn't complete its first season because of financial struggles and a management committee that wasn't forceful enough with clubs, leaving most of those clubs with their own financial issues. Broxburn FC were no exception and in 1894 the original club folded because of the pressures.

They re-formed as Broxburn Football Club in 1901 but, during the seven-year period between their folding and re-forming, the town's football banner had been carried by Broxburn Shamrock. In 1904 both Broxburn clubs joined the re-formed Eastern League and after a season both moved on to the Scottish Football Alliance. While this was going on another Broxburn club arrived on the scene, Broxburn Athletic. They entered the Eastern League until 1907, when they moved to the Central League.

By 1911 Broxburn had three teams playing in a range of Scottish football non-league set-ups. Shamrock were in the Eastern League, Athletic were plying their trade in the Central League, while Broxburn FC were in the Scottish Football Union. In the spring of 1912, Broxburn FC moved from the Union to join Broxburn Athletic in the Central League. Then a few months later it was announced that Broxburn FC and Broxburn Athletic would merge to form Broxburn United Football Club. It was considered more sensible for the small town's teams to pull their resources together and put up a bigger challenge than play separately.

Broxburn United had a solid run up to the outbreak of the First World War, staying in the Central League until 1915, then joining the Eastern League. While things were on the up for United, Broxburn Shamrock started to drift away and by the outbreak of war they were no longer playing in any formal league and had stopped applying to enter any cups. With the outbreak of war, Shamrock suspended most of their actions and when in 1919 the leagues returned, Broxburn Shamrock didn't and ceased as a company shortly afterwards.

Meanwhile, Broxburn United re-joined the Central League after the war, staying in it until 1921, when the Central League was absorbed into the SFL as the new Second Division. United opened their account with a 3-1 defeat of Dunfermline Athletic at home in front of just under 4,000 spectators. This momentum continued for most of the season and they ended in a very respectable seventh place. The following season was just as impressive, as they won 14 matches and came eighth.

United's third season wasn't as successful after they had made a bad start to the campaign. However, their form picked up a bit towards the end, which was just enough for them to finish three points above the drop zone, in 15th place. The 1924/25 season was a vast improvement. They made a very strong start, but at the turn of the year their form slipped, finishing in seventh again.

United's final season in the SFL was in 1925/26. They got off to a bad start, losing a closely fought match 1-0 to King's Park before being smashed 8-0 by St Bernard's. After that they never really improved and by February were cut adrift at the bottom with little hope of anything changing.

While the play on the park was bad, off of it an interesting story was developing.

In February 1926 they hosted league leaders Stenhousemuir. After the match, Stenny goalkeeper Joe Shortt came forward to say that a Glasgow bookie had offered him £50 to lose the match. The league investigated but found no evidence that Broxburn had anything to do with it. Not that it mattered a great deal, as United lost the match 2-1.

The rest of the season didn't improve and United recorded just four wins altogether. As the Third Division had been called off just a few weeks before, this saved them from the financial quagmire of that division. However, they instead had to face the uncertainty of a re-election vote, which unfortunately was unsuccessful, so they left the league that season.

Broxburn United joined most of the clubs from the old Third Division in entering the Scottish Football Alliance, but with their attendances low and with the overall economic environment, after just one season United moved into the junior ranks from 1927/28. But by 1931/32 even this was a step too far for them, and finally in 1932 the club folded, with cash flow the main contributing factor.

After the Second World War, in 1947, some local businessmen came together and formed a new Broxburn Athletic Football Club. They have been successful in the junior ranks and since 2018 have been a senior club, now plying their trade in the East of Scotland League.

4. Clackmannan

The small historical town of Clackmannan was the county town of Clackmannanshire until 1812, when the growth and development of Alloa led to it taking over that role. Clackmannan Football Club formed in 1885 following on from the success of nearby Alloa Athletic FC. In their early years Clackmannan spent their time moving around grounds throughout the town before settling at Chapelhill Park. During the time prior to joining a league they took to playing in local cups and friendlies.

When the SFL was formed, many other leagues popped up around the country, one of which was the Midland League formed in 1891. This was a league made up of clubs predominantly from Fife, Stirling and Clackmannanshire. During the league's first season Clackmannan FC beat Dunfermline Athletic 17-2 in what's still Dunfermline's record defeat.

Clackmannan would remain in the Midland League, including winning it in 1896/97, until 1898, when they moved into the Central Combination. By 1908 they were back in the Midland League, staying until 1912 when they moved to the Eastern League.

At the outbreak of the First World War, Clackmannan were comfortable members of the Eastern League, but when that league was suspended in 1915 they joined the Central League. However, this was only in name at that stage as they didn't get to play in the league until it restarted in 1919.

The SFL re-formed its Second Division in 1921, made up of the teams from the Western, Eastern and Central Leagues. Clackmannan were one of those lucky clubs, and for the 1921/22 season the tiny town of 3,000 people had a team in the SFL second tier. That season was a mixed bag for the county of Clackmannanshire. At the one end, Alloa Athletic won the

Second Division title and became the first team to be promoted to the top flight through automatic promotion in Scotland, while at the other end were Clackmannan, who, despite winning nine matches, finished bottom of the league. Under normal circumstances they would have faced a re-election vote, but it was decided to reduce the number of teams in the Second Division, so Clackmannan and Dundee Hibernian were out of the league without the opportunity to seek re-election.

Clackmannan entered the Eastern League for 1922/23 and had a successful season, finishing in the top three. They then prepared a bid to return to the SFL Second Division in the spring of 1923, which was unsuccessful. However, this wasn't the end of their chances of getting league football, as in the summer of 1923 the SFL announced that a Third Division was to be formed.

Clackmannan's time in the Third Division was very much a mid-table existence. They spent their second spell in the SFL in this division, finishing in 12th, 10th and 15th. Like many of the clubs at that time, they were struggling to keep up the guarantee payments, although this wasn't as crippling for them as it was several others. Their issue was more the small population and the instability of the league's financial position, which ruined the league football dream of Clackmannan FC.

By the second half of 1925/26, the league campaign was abandoned as the Third Division collapsed, with Clackmannan in 15th place. Following this, they were one of the few clubs not entering the Scottish Football Alliance, instead opting to play in just the Scottish Cup and friendlies for the time being.

After several first-round exits from the Scottish Cup, Clackmannan finally closed down in 1931, as the finances needed to have a successful league team weren't available to a club whose average gate was under 400; that and the overall economic situation throughout the country made things even harder for such clubs to carry on.

As for the town, a junior team played there between 1962 and 1995, but since then no other team has come from the town. Most of the locals travel to nearby Alloa Athletic. These days an estate has been built on the former ground, Chapelhill, and a road in the estate runs roughly through the middle of the old pitch.

5. Dykehead

Dykehead is part of the mining town of Shotts, which lies near enough halfway between Glasgow and Edinburgh and is known for its ironworks and mining. The town was at its height in the decade before the Second World War with 22 mines in the local area, the last of these closing in the 1960s.

Dykehead Football Club formed in 1880 and played in friendlies and unofficial local cups until 1884, when they gained SFA membership and entered the Scottish Cup for the first time, losing 5-2 in the first round to Wishaw Swifts. Over the next couple of seasons, they were knocked out of the cup in heavy defeats, 7-0 and 8-0 to Albion Rovers and Airdrieonians, respectively.

Dykehead joined the Scottish Football Alliance in 1895, but after just one season they left and entered more local leagues for a couple of seasons until 1898 when they joined the Scottish Football Federation. By 1905 they were on the move again, this time to the Scottish Football Combination until 1909, when they joined the Scottish Football Union. In the Union they won the title in 1912/13, and remained in that league until its suspension in 1915 because of the First World War.

In 1915 Dykehead moved to the Western League but after two seasons withdrew due to the war and the demands put upon the mining town's people, which made attracting spectators nearly impossible. At the war's end they re-entered the Western League, remaining there until 1923 when the SFL incorporated the Western League into its new Third Division.

Dykehead's first season in the Third Division was a rather successful one, ending it in fifth place after winning 13 of 15 matches at home, although to counter this, losing 12 away matches. The following couple of seasons were marked more by financial problems than on-field success. The 1924/25 season saw them abandon two matches because they simply couldn't meet the £15 match guarantee, and on countless occasions they were given warnings about delayed payment of the guarantee to their visitors. On the pitch, 1924/25 saw them slump to 12th in the league.

In the following season, 1925/26, Dykehead's off-field position was just as perilous. They barely took the required £15 so the owners often dipped into their own pockets to meet the guarantee requirements. On the pitch, on the other hand, they had a much better season, and when in April the league was abandoned, they were in fourth place.

When the league was called off, Dykehead were an outside contender to be retained in the SFL but, unfortunately, the club's financial state was never one that would cope with the monetary needs of the league above. So, it came as no surprise that they weren't voted into the Second Division.

After this failure at the AGM vote, Dykehead entered the Scottish Football Alliance for one season, then moved on to the Provincial League, but again left after a year. Their last official match was against Hibs in the Scottish Cup in January 1928. However, Dykehead failed to turn up so Hibs were awarded a walkover.

The club sadly folded early in 1928. The mix of the disaster of the league campaign and the downturn in the economic circumstances around the mining industry hit the town. Plus, with people moving to the town from the cities of Edinburgh and Glasgow, on Saturdays they would rather travel out to the cities to watch the more successful teams than watch a small struggling local one.

For the town, no team played at any level outside that of amateur until 1950, when Shotts Bon Accord Football Club formed as a junior club. They went on to be successful, including winning the Scottish Junior Cup twice, and in 2020 became a senior club, entering the West of Scotland League, with a route back to the SPFL.

Current Clubs

THERE ARE several current clubs playing in a variety of leagues who at one point had a representative in the SFL. Some of these have simply had a name change over time and have never had a break in membership; others dropped down to the junior ranks. Arguably the most well-known story is that of Ayr United Football Club, formed in 1910 after a merger between the two league teams from Ayr. Ayr Football Club, founded in 1879, were already a club formed from mergers of two other clubs. The first was Ayr Thistle Football Club, formed in 1872 and a team that had reached the 1877 Scottish Cup semi-final, being knocked out 9-0 by Vale of Leven. The other founding club of Ayr FC was Ayr Academicals Football Club, founded in 1876 after the merger of two other small clubs in Ayr Academy Football Club and Ayr Eglinton Football Club. Little is known of the two clubs that formed Ayr Academicals FC; they never entered the Scottish Cup and Ayr Academicals were viewed very much as the smaller of the two Ayr clubs of the time.

In 1879, Ayr Thistle and Ayr Academicals came together to try to form a stronger team to challenge the dominance of the Glasgow clubs. At the time there were five teams playing in Ayr, so for Ayr FC to become the most prominent team in the town would require hard work and good marketing. This was helped massively by the connection Ayr Thistle had to prominent English club Aston Villa. In 1878, Archie Hunter left Ayr Thistle to originally join Calthorpe FC in Birmingham. When he couldn't locate them, he was persuaded to join Aston Villa instead because of their large contingent of Scottish players. Hunter would go on to become a household name for his dribbling and gentlemanly conduct on the pitch. He would also be the Aston Villa captain that led the team to its first FA Cup win. He never forgot his roots, though, and during his time at Villa they played Ayr on four occasions, three times in Ayr, one of which was a 3-0 victory for Ayr at the opening of New Somerset Park. Hunter, who is still Aston Villa's record FA Cup goalscorer, had a heart attack during a league match against Everton in 1890 and died a few years later from pneumonia in 1894. He was 35 years old.

Ayr FC made the most of their connections and played a lot of glamour friendlies, including in 1888 taking on and beating Canada 4-0 at Somerset Park and going on a tour of Ireland. By the 1890s, they had made themselves the strongest team in the town. They also have a respectable Scottish Cup record and joined the Scottish Football Alliance in 1891/92. When professionalism was finally allowed in Scotland, Ayr FC joined the Ayrshire Combination League, winning it three out of four years. After a few rejections in applications to join the SFL, they finally made it into the Second Division for the 1897/98 season.

Over the next 13 seasons, Ayr FC were a constant fixture in the Second Division. At no point did they ever drop below mid-table, therefore never having to face the uncertainty of a re-election vote. During the mid-1900s they finished third three times but never went any higher. By 1906, they had been joined by their follow Ayr team Ayr Parkhouse.

Ayr Parkhouse Football Club formed in 1886 and took their name from the club's training ground. They moved into Beresford Park in 1888 when their rivals Ayr FC vacated the ground and moved to Somerset Park.

Ayr Parkhouse adhered strictly to their amateur status when others in the town became professional. They played in the Ayrshire Football Combination from 1893, but after Ayr FC's successful move into the SFL's Second Division in 1897, they became determined to try to gain SFA membership and a league position. By the turn of the century, they were the best of the amateur teams without SFA membership.

Finally, by 1903, Ayr Parkhouse achieved their goal and gained membership of the Second Division. However, that season was nothing shy of a disaster. They lost 15 matches and finished bottom. When the re-election came around, they were voted out in favour of Aberdeen, so they dropped back into the Ayrshire Football Combination.

After two seasons in the local leagues, Parkhouse were voted back into the Second Division for the 1906/07 season. Again they finished bottom but this time survived the vote. Season 1907/08 was the definition of mid-table. They finished sixth out of 12 team, ending the season with a record of:

P	W	D	L	F	A	Pts
22	11	0	11	38	38	22

With another mid-table finish in 1908/09, Parkhouse entered the 1909/10 season looking like a semi-reliable team.

However, the season was a disaster and it became clear that the town of Ayr couldn't cope with two league clubs. Neither had the money to make a big impact on the league but it was hoped that if they came together that might change.

So, towards the end of the 1909/10 season, Parkhouse made the first tentative steps towards the two clubs merging and, after a small amount of persuasion, Ayr FC and Ayr Parkhouse concluded that being as one would work better than being separate. By June 1910 it was announced that the two clubs had merged as Ayr United Football Club.

Good results soon came for the new team and they finished second in 1910/11. They then went one better in winning the league in their next two seasons, before being voted into the First Division for 1913/14.

Since that day, Ayr United have been a constant in the upper leagues of Scottish football and have gone on to create their own history, but few remember that an actual derby took place in the SFL in the small seaside town of Ayr.

* * *

Dundee Hibernians are well known due to their success once they were renamed Dundee United in October 1923. The original club formed in 1909 and entered the Second Division in 1910, where they remained until 1915 when the league was suspended. They then spent time in the Eastern Division until 1921, when the Second Division was re-formed. That season was a shocker for Dundee Hibernians as they dropped out of the league because of its restructure.

After a season in the local leagues, they successfully reapplied to join the second tier. Not long afterwards they looked to change their name in an attempt to put some distance between themselves and their Irish connections. This was in response to the political climate of the time and to open the club up to more supporters from different backgrounds. They first wanted to be known as Dundee City but after Dundee protested it was agreed that Dundee United would be the club's name.

Since the name change in October 1923 Dundee United have gone from strength to strength and in 1983 won the SFL. Since that league triumph they have also contested eight Scottish Cup finals, winning twice.

* * *

The year 1923 has provided so many of the forgotten clubs in this book. Most that entered the Third Division that season left by 1926 and folded within a few years of the league ending. However, there are a few that have kept on going without coming back into the league.

One of those clubs came from the small historical coastal town of Peebles near the English border. Peebles Rovers Football Club formed in 1893 and stuck to playing against local teams until 1907, when they entered the Scottish Cup for the first time, losing to Celtic 4-0. In 1909 they entered and won the Scottish Football Union, then for the following season joined the Eastern League. With a few years of success behind them, they attempted to join the SFL but failed on each occasion.

With the coming of the First World War Peebles Rovers suspended most of their activities and wouldn't play in a league again until 1919 when they joined the Borders League. After just two seasons they joined the Eastern League for a season, before moving on in 1922/23 to the Western League. In the summer of 1923, 11 of the 12 clubs in the Western League were moved into the newly formed SFL Third Division. Peebles Rovers were one of these clubs and, as such, became an official SFL team.

They spent three seasons in the league, ending with two bottom-three finishes sandwiching a high of eighth place. By the time the 1925/26 season was suspended, they were 14th of 16 teams and their time within the SFL came to an end.

After the disappointment of the Third Division, Peebles Rovers returned to their roots in the East of Scotland League, winning it five times over the next nine seasons. After the Second World War they won the league title one more time and remained strong finishers, before slowly starting to decline in the early 1960s. By 1966/67 they had ended in junior football and declined further before, in 1980, re-joining the senior ranks and entering the East of Scotland League again. Since then, they have been on the rise, and now have a clear route back to the SPFL.

* * *

The other club that survived the collapse of the Third Division but never came back were from the small town of Larkhall. Royal Albert Football Club formed in 1878 from two local pit teams. During their first 50 years they were a constant feature of the lower non-league divisions and in 1890 even got through to the fifth round of the Scottish Cup, losing 5-0 to Celtic. They were also the first team to be awarded a penalty in Scotland, on 6 June 1891, in a local cup tie against Airdrieonians, with James McLuggage scoring it.

In 1891 Royal Albert helped form the Scottish Federation but after two seasons and winning it in the second of those, they left and joined the Scottish Football Alliance in 1893. They won the Alliance in their first season and applied for election to the SFL. Unfortunately, they were unsuccessful. After another couple of strong seasons, they left the Alliance and became a founding member of the Scottish Football Combination. Royal Albert remained in the Combination for the next ten seasons, including winning it in 1903/04. They made three attempts to be elected to the SFL but on each occasion they couldn't muster the support from the other clubs.

In 1906, after their third election failure, Royal Albert took the strange decision to move from the Combination to the Scottish Football Union. This was an odd move as that league was made up mostly of the reserve teams from the SFL, so the quality of the league was never particularly high. They stayed in the Union until 1915 but, when the SFL Second Division was suspended due to the war, Royal Albert saw the opportunity and moved into the Western Division with many former league clubs.

Finally, in 1923 Royal Albert, along with most of the Western League, became founder members of the SFL Third Division. Their time in the SFL was short-lived, however. After a couple of ninth-place finishes they improved in their final season to fifth, but then the league was called off. After a few weeks it was announced those clubs in the suspended league would lose their membership.

After this, Royal Albert wound up as a senior club and re-formed as a junior one, retaining everything they had at the senior level. They made a name as a junior club, playing in Larkhall until 2013 when they moved over to nearby Stonehouse due to losing their ground because of redevelopment. Today, they are in the lower echelons of the West of Scotland League with a route back to the SPFL.

* * *

The final club in this round-up is Meadowbank Thistle, better known as Livingston Football Club, when they changed their name after moving from Edinburgh to Livingston.

Meadowbank Thistle started off in the 1940s as Ferranti Thistle, a works team from Ferranti Engineering works. They started off playing in the amateur leagues around the Edinburgh area and were one of the strongest amateur teams in the country. In 1953 they joined the senior game and the East of Scotland League, where they would remain until an SFL restructure in 1974, following the demise of Third Lanark. That year Ferranti Thistle applied for the vacant place and beat Inverness Thistle in a tight vote, 21 to 16.

For the club to join the league they needed to change their name, as the SFL had a rule against such sponsorship in a club's name. So, Ferranti Thistle became Meadowbank Thistle, named after the stadium they played in. They have since remained in the league, mostly bouncing around the second and third tiers. They faced financial trouble in the early 1990s and announced that they would need to move to Livingston and have since, as Livingston, made their own history. After some bumps in the road, they have settled into their current home and seem to have a stable future ahead.

Bibliography

David Potter & Phil H Jones: *The History of the Scottish Cup, The Story of Every Season 1873-2016*. Pitch Publishing 2016

Bob Crampsey: *The First 100 Years*. The Scottish Football League 1990

Scott Burns: *Scottish Football, It's Not All About the Old Firm*. Pitch Publishing 2012

Archie Hunter: *Triumphs Of The Football Field*. Birmingham Weekly Mercury 1890, Re-Published Sports Projects Ltd 1997

Robin Holmes: *Forgotten: Scotland's Former Football League Clubs*. Independently published 2020

Gary Sutherland: *Hunting Grounds, Scottish Football Safari*. Birlinn 2007

Anton Hodge: *In Black and White: The Rise, Fall and Rebirth of Gretna Football*. Chequered Flag Publishing 2015

Andrew Ross: *Gretna FC Living The Dream*. Black and White Publishing 2007

Hugh Keevins & Kevin McCarra: *100 Cups, The Story of The Scottish Cup*. Mainstream Publishing Company 1985

John Rafferty: *One Hundred Years of Scottish Football*. Pan Books Ltd 1973

Bob Crampsey: *The Scottish Footballer.* William
   Blackwood & Sons 1978
Alan Breck: *Alan Breck's Book of Scottish Football.* Scottish
   Daily Express Publications 1937
Bob Crampsey: *The Game for The Game's Sake, The
   History of Queen's Park Football Club.* The Queen's Park
   Football Club 1967

Various newspaper archives, including the *Glasgow Times, The
Herald, The Daily Record, The Scottish Daily Mail* and a variety
of others that are now defunct.

Also available at all good book stores

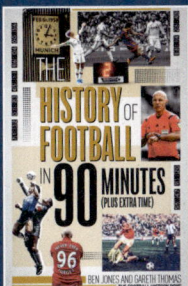

9781785318399

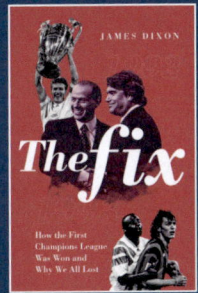

9781785317781

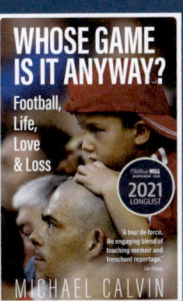

9781785318849

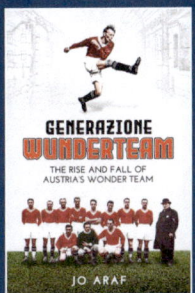

9781785318528

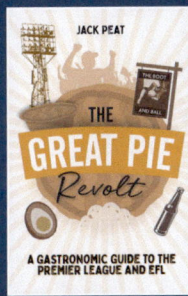

9781785316722

9781785317576

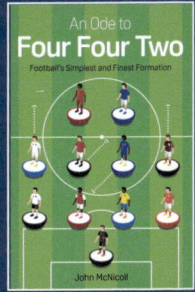

9781785318382

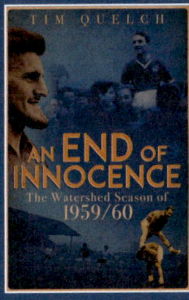

9781785317583

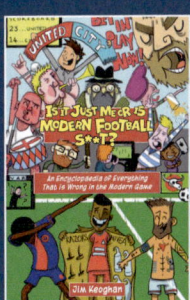

9781785317736